DAY 1

Abba Father we come to You in humility before Your royal throne. We come to You collectively bringing our prayers and supplications before You, with thankfulness in our hearts and mouths. We first ask for forgiveness for anything we have done that was displaying in Your sight. We appeal to You on behalf of our brothers and sisters and our ancestors. We ask that You have grace and mercy on us and on them. Your word says if we seek You first and acknowledge You in all of our ways You will direct our paths. We come before You with obedient and serving hearts that long to abide in Your word and give You glory in everything we do. Please direct us Father. We come to You first seeking your kingdom in hopes that our every need and desire will be added into us because our needs are met by You, the great provider, and our desires are that Your will be done in us and through us.

Let our mouths be full of wisdom and allow kindness to always be on our tongues. We pray that you release the Holy spirit upon us to quicken our spirits with Your purifying fire. Burn up any impurities that may exist in us Father. Remind us to always act selflessly and without conceit. Help us to walk in humility and always love others as we love You, better than we love ourselves. Help us to be righteous examples of Your love Father. Help us to be righteous representatives of Your fruit. We pray that our light shines and displays Your glory wherever we go. That when people look at us they see You. That when they hear our words they hear Your voice. When they see our works they see Your hand. Let there be less of us daily and more of You in everything we do. Help us to not forget who we serve and whose we are. Allow us not to be moved by the favor of men, and not to search for it. Allow us not to be moved by not being accepted by the world, and not long for acceptance from anyone but You. Allow us not to be moved when rejected by family and so called friends, but to embrace those who walk after Your righteousness as our true family. Keep our hearts and minds on one accord and in the likeness of the Messiah, always abounding in obedience and graciousness. Fortify us in Your strength Father in the face of every adversity. Your word says that the weapons that form against us will not prosper because You will be with us wherever we go. We put on the armor You have provided for us in this time of battle, reminding us that this battle is not against flesh and blood but against principalities and powers, and wickedness that we have been given the victory over in You through our obedience to Your will. Keep our feet shod in the preparation of peace, that we always be covered in the peace that surpasses our own understanding. Let our heads be covered with the helmet of salvation constantly keeping our minds in the part of obedience and reminding us to execute that which we have studied pertaining to life and godliness. Let us always have on the breastplate of righteousness for the treasures of wickedness profit nothing: but righteousness delivereth from death, knowing that Your eyes are upon the righteous, and Your ears are open unto their cry.

Let us be girded in truth because You are near all that call upon You in truth and they that deal truly are Your delight. And lastly let us take up the sword of the spirit which is Your word which sanctifies us through the truth because Your word is truth. And also the shield of faith for it is by faith we walk and not by sight and it is in faith that the battles are won, and the enemies attempts are overcome. We thank You for these provisions as we go forth this day. Remind us to stay focused on those things which are good, pure, perfect, true, just, honest, lovely, and of good report. Remind us to stay in the mind of praise for it is in the praise that You are glorified and your magnificent works are proclaimed. We will not fear nor will we be discouraged. We know who our help is. We know who our provider is. We know who our protector is. We know that this is Providence and our end is expected. We will let Your perfect peace reign in our hearts with the honor that we have been chosen for this, your marvelous work and that which has been started will be completed in us. We love you Father. We thank You for choosing us and loving us, for forgiving us, and perfecting us, for using us, and for filling us to overflow with all you have for us. We bless your holy name. It is written and we claim it as done. So be it.

Matthew 6:33-34 But seek ye first the kingdom of God, and his righteousness; and all these things shall be added unto you. Take therefore no thought for the morrow: for the morrow shall take thought for the things of itself. Sufficient unto the day is the evil thereof.

Proverbs 31:26 She openeth her mouth with wisdom; and in her tongue is the law of kindness.

Philippians 2:3-5 Let nothing be done through strife or vainglory; but in lowliness of mind let each esteem other better than themselves. Look not every man on his own things, but every man also on the things of others. Let this mind be in you, which was also in Christ Jesus:

Galatians 1:10 For do I now persuade men, or God? or do I seek to please men? for if I yet pleased men, I should not be the servant of Christ?

Ephesians 6:11-18 Put on the whole armour of God, that ye may be able to stand against the wiles of the devil. For we wrestle not against flesh and blood, but against principalities, against powers, against the rulers of the darkness of this world, against spiritual wickedness in high places. Wherefore take unto you the whole armour of God, that ye may be able to withstand in the evil day, and having done all, to stand. Stand therefore, having your loins girt about with truth, and having on the breastplate of righteousness; And your feet shod with the preparation of the gospel of peace; Above all, taking the shield of faith, wherewith ye shall be able to quench all the fiery darts of the wicked. And take the helmet of salvation, and the sword of the Spirit, which is the word of God: Praying always with all prayer and supplication in the Spirit, and watching thereunto with all perseverance and supplication for all saints

Phillipians 4:6-8 Be careful for nothing; but in every thing by prayer and supplication with thanksgiving let your requests be made known unto God. And the peace of God, which passeth all understanding, shall keep your hearts and minds through Christ Jesus. Finally, brethren, whatsoever things are true, whatsoever things are honest, whatsoever things are just, whatsoever things are pure, whatsoever things are lovely, whatsoever things are of good report; if there be any virtue, and if there be any praise, think on these things.

Proverbs 10:2 Treasures of wickedness profit nothing: but righteousness delivereth from death.

Psalm 34:15 The eyes of the LORD are upon the righteous, and his ears are open unto their cry.

Psalms 145:18 The LORD is nigh unto all them that call upon him, to all that call upon him in truth.

Proverbs 12:22 Lying lips are abomination to the LORD: but they that deal truly are his delight

John 17:17 Sanctify them through thy truth: thy word is truth.

Jeremiah 29:11 For I know the thoughts that I think toward you, saith the LORD, thoughts of peace, and not of evil, to give you an expected end.

2 Corinthians 5:7 For we walk by faith, not by sight

Joshua 1:9 Have not I commanded thee? Be strong and of a

good courage; be not afraid, neither be thou dismayed: for the LORD thy God is with thee whithersoever thou goest.

Colossians 3:12-15 Put on therefore, as the elect of God, holy and beloved, bowels of mercies, kindness, humbleness of mind, meekness, longsuffering; Forbearing one another, and forgiving one another, if any man have a quarrel against any: even as Christ forgave you, so also do ye. And above all these things put on charity, which is the bond of perfectness. And let the peace of God rule in your hearts, to the which also ye are called in one body; and be ye thankful.

DAY 2

Heavenly Father we come boldly unto Your throne of grace, that we may obtain mercy, and find grace to help us in our time of need. We come before You on one accord because we know that where two or three are gathered together in Your name, You are in the midst of them. We ask for forgiveness Father for anything we have done that displeased You. Correct us Father for we know that those whom You love You chasten. We ask for forgiveness on behalf of our nation Father. We ask that You show Your loving kindness and correction to them as well. Help us to be what You created us to be. Our hearts rejoice in You. There is none holy as You Father: for there is none beside You neither is there any rock like our Elohim. Let us not be proud or let arrogancy come out of our mouths for the Most High is a God of knowledge, and by Him actions are weighed. The weapons of the strong are broken, and they that stumble are girded with strength. Father, You alone are the giver and taker of life. You alone control who is poor, and rich: You bringeth low, and lifteth up. You alone have the power to raise up the poor out of the dust, and to set them among princes, and to make them inherit the throne of glory: for the pillars of the earth are the Most High's, and You hath set the world upon them.You keep the feet of Your saints, and the wicked shall be silent in darkness. Without Your strength we cannot succeed. Our adversaries will be broken to pieces because our adversaries are Your adversaries. Help us to stand in Your strength until the time of judgement comes. Enlarge our territory Father. Increase the capacity of the light that shines through us and those that it reaches. We pray that Your hand forever be with us keeping us from wickedness. Because You alone are a shield for us, and the lifter up of our head. In You we have no shame or condemnation . We cry to You with one voice, praying that You will hear our cries. We rest assured because You sustain us. We will not be afraid of ten thousands of people that have set themselves against us and surround us. We live in the land of the enemy but this world is Yours and all of it must submit to You, Our Power. Let Your Power Arise, Father and come to our defense because Your word says that You will fight for us and avenge us. Salvation belongs to You, and we ask that You bless us Your chosen children. Allow us to always be a blessing. Allow us to walk in wisdom towards them that have none. Let our speech be gracious and seasoned with salt Father. Govern our mouths and let us speak with patience so that we may have the time for the Holy spirit to direct our thoughts. Bless us with wisdom and understanding Father. Let every word that proceeds from our mouths be spoken in wisdom and truth. Let every word glorify You. Your word says for us not to forsake wisdom and she will preserve us, love her and she shall keep us. Exalt her and she will promote us, embrace her and she will bring us to honor. So we implore You Ruach come to us and never leave us and we will never leave you. We exalt you, we embrace you, we love you Wisdom. Bless us with Your understanding as we forsake our own. Lead us in your ways and impart to us what you will have us to know and the words you will have us to speak at the appointed time. Calm us when we are anxious, quiet our mouths when we need to be silent, direct our paths and order our steps when we should move. Send us Your spirit to lead, guide and direct us in Your ways Father that we may be pleasing in Your sight. So that we may be seen fit to wear the crown of glory wisdom provides and that she will bless our heads with the ornament of grace. Assist us through Your Holy Spirit in producing Your fruits of love, peace, long suffering, gentleness, goodness, faith, meekness, and temperance. Help us to walk in the characteristics of wisdom with purity without favoritism or fakeness. Help us to be slow to anger as we obtain self control through the understanding she brings us. Blessed be the name of the Most High for ever and ever, for wisdom and might are Yours alone. We thank you that every petition we have brought before You will be granted to us according to Your riches and glory Father. We pray that You will magnify us so that Your power and glory will shine before all men. We thank and praise You Father for You alone are worthy to be praised. We wait with expectancy of the affirmative of our prayers. We give You honor and glory. We claim these things because it is written and it is done. So be it.

Matthew 18:20 For where two or three are gathered together in my name, there am I in the midst of them.

1Samuel 2:1-10 1And Hannah prayed, and said, My heart rejoiceth in the Lord, mine horn is exalted in the Lord: my mouth is enlarged over mine enemies; because I rejoice in thy salvation.There is none holy as the Lord: for there is none beside thee: neither is there any rock like our God.Talk no more so exceeding proudly; let not arrogancy come out of your mouth: for the Lord is a God of knowledge, and by him actions are weighed.The bows of the mighty men are broken, and they that stumbled are girded with strength.They that were full have hired out themselves for bread; and they that were hungry ceased: so that the barren hath born seven; and she that hath many children is waxed feeble.The Lord killeth, and maketh alive: he bringeth down to the grave, and bringeth up.The Lord maketh poor, and maketh rich: he bringeth low, and lifteth up.He raiseth up the poor out of the dust, and lifteth up the beggar from the dunghill, to set them among princes, and to make them inherit the throne of glory: for the pillars of the earth are the Lord's, and he hath set the world upon them.He will keep the feet of his saints, and the wicked shall be silent in darkness; for by strength shall no man prevail.The adversaries of the Lord shall be broken to pieces; out of heaven shall he thunder upon them: the Lord shall judge the ends of the earth; and he shall give strength unto his king, and exalt the horn of his anointed.

Hebrews 12:6-7 For whom the Lord loveth he chasteneth, and scourgeth every son whom he receiveth. If ye endure chastening, God dealeth with you as with sons; for what son is

he whom the father chasteneth not?

Hebrews 4:16 Let us therefore come boldly unto the throne of grace, that we may obtain mercy, and find grace to help in time of need

Colossians 4:5-6 Walk in wisdom toward them that are without, redeeming the time. Let your speech be always with grace, seasoned with salt, that ye may know how ye ought to answer every man.

Proverbs 4:5-9 Get wisdom, get understanding: forget it not; neither decline from the words of my mouth. Forsake her not, and she shall preserve thee: love her, and she shall keep thee. Wisdom is the principal thing; therefore get wisdom: and with all thy getting get understanding. Exalt her, and she shall promote thee: she shall bring thee to honour, when thou dost embrace her. She shall give to thine head an ornament of grace: a crown of glory shall she deliver to thee.

Galatians 5:22-23 But the fruit of the Spirit is love, joy, peace, longsuffering, gentleness, goodness, faith, Meekness, temperance: against such there is no law.

James 3:17 But the wisdom that is from above is first pure, then peaceable, gentle, and easy to be entreated, full of mercy and good fruits, without partiality, and without hypocrisy.

Proverbs 14:29 He that is slow to wrath is of great understanding: but he that is hasty of spirit exalteth folly.

Daniel 2:20 Daniel answered and said, Blessed be the name of God for ever and ever: for wisdom and might are his:

1Chronicles 4:10 And Jabez called on the God of Israel, saying, Oh that thou wouldest bless me indeed, and enlarge my coast, and that thine hand might be with me, and that thou wouldest keep me from evil, that it may not grieve me! And God granted him that which he requested.

Psalms 3 Lord, how are they increased that trouble me! many are they that rise up against me. Many there be which say of my soul, There is no help for him in God. Selah. But thou, O Lord, art a shield for me; my glory, and the lifter up of mine head. I cried unto the Lord with my voice, and he heard me out of his holy hill. Selah. I laid me down and slept; I awaked; for the Lord sustained me. I will not be afraid of ten thousands of people, that have set themselves against me round about. Arise, O Lord; save me, O my God: for thou hast smitten all mine enemies upon the cheek bone; thou hast broken the teeth of the ungodly. Salvation belongeth unto the Lord: thy blessing is upon thy people. Selah.

DAY 3

Abba we come before You today with Thanksgiving in our hearts and praise in our mouths for You are worthy to receive all the praise and glory. We adore You Father. We thank you for providing for us. We thank You for protecting us. We thank You for proving us and trying us. We know these trials are a testing of our faith which produces patience in us. We thank You that everything works together for the good of us who love You Father and we do love You Father.

We love You because You loved us when we didn't even love ourselves. You never gave up on us Father and we are forever grateful. Father we could never be worthy of Your consideration of us but we are grateful that You choose to do it anyway. We ask that You forgive us for every thought and every act that was not in line with Your will. Forgive us for displeasing You. Forgive us for not living up to the standard You have set for us. We ask for forgiveness on behalf of our nation, and on behalf of our ancestors. Bless us with a spirit of obedience and reverence Father. Give us the ability to listen and heed Your voice. Give us the wisdom and knowledge to walk in Your ways at all times. Give us the eyes to see Your truth in all things. Give us the ability to conquer our flesh when it rises up and to stay in the spirit. Help us to respond with the peace that passes all understanding. Help us to react with love and kindness and to walk in temperance . Help us to overcome anger with goodness and love. . We ask that You give us supernatural favor and go before us in every situation to make light the way. Allow us to build up and not tear down. Help us to be gracious and edifying in our speech at all times. We pray that we will be the wives You have called us to be. Let us be the mothers, and nurturers You created is to be. Let us be the beacons of light that shine against every darkness that rises against Your will Father. Help us to be the vessels we need to be for You to gain all the glory in everything we do. Let Your face and love be seen in our actions. Keep us from all wickedness Father. We pray that every attack of the enemy will be rendered void against us. Father we pray that every tongue, every hand, every weapon that comes against us in adversity be cast down. We claim that no weapon formed against us will prosper. Your word says that what is loosed on earth is loosed in heaven therefore Father we lose the power of the holy spirit to minister to us, to teach us, and order our steps. We lose the warring angels to defend and fight on our behalf. Keep us from the demons of worry, anxiety, doubt, fear, anger, jealousy, depression, hate, grudge holding, condemnation , guilt, shame, disobedience, greed, lust and any other unrighteous demon that would seek to attach itself to us and keep us from being used by You and resting in You. We ask that you protect our families. Keep the demons of dissention, disruption, confusion, disrespect, envy, derision, pride, accusation, and contempt from abiding in our homes. Let the seeds that have been planted in those that are still sleeping begin to take root. Help us to have patience and act with love when dealing with those who are still in bondage. Let our children love one another and let our homes be filled with Your presence and Your love. Father we ask that You will give us the strength to continue through each day. Give us the ability to complete every task You put before us. Make it clear to us what is priority and what is our concern. Help us to know the difference between Your business and our business. Give us the ability to let You be Sovereign. Remind us that You don't need our help doing Your job as our Awesome Father. Keep us in mind that YOU are our provider, our protector, and our portion. That with You for us none can be against us. Comfort us Father and allow us the ability to wait on You. We ask these things with great expectancy that our desires will be met for we know that these requests will bring You all of the glory. We thank You in advance. We give You the glory and the honor. We claim the victory in every battle and we claim our blessings as the privilege of being Your chosen daughters. We believe we shall receive it and we shall have it for it is written and it is already done. So be it.

Isaiah 54:17 No weapon that is formed against thee shall prosper; and every tongue that shall rise against thee in judgment thou shalt condemn. This is the heritage of the servants of the Lord, and their righteousness is of me, saith the Lord.

Matthew 18:18Verily I say unto you, Whatsoever ye shall bind on earth shall be bound in heaven: and whatsoever ye shall loose on earth shall be loosed in heaven.

Mark 11:24 Therefore I say unto you, What things soever ye desire, when ye pray, believe that ye receive them, and ye shall have them.

DAY 4

Dearest Heavenly Father we come to You with praise on our lips. We thank You for the Mountains that You are moving in our lives. We thank You for this trial period. We thank You for the preparation for what's to come. Father thank You for taking the time to prove our faith with Your purifying fire. Thank You for taking the time to chasten us and purge us of all unrighteousness. We know that it is because of Your undying love for us that you correct us and cleanse us of all unrighteousness. We thank You for this day, for this opportunity to continue our walk in Your perfect will. We thank You for every experience You have allowed us to have that gives us wisdom and produces the patience that strengthens our endurance. Thank You for being sovereign over our lives and all things. Thank You father for giving us the opportunity to be still and come to know You as the Most High God of Israel Creator of All Things. Thank You for Your strategic planning that fortified us in the areas where You know we will falter without You. We ask You for forgiveness for every unrighteous deed, every unrighteous thought, every unrighteous action that we have displayed. Let us not tarnish Your name anymore Father. Give us the ability to walk in the perfection You created us to mirror. Give us the ability to stop trying to take over Your work and to successfully accomplish the work You have placed before us. Father we ask that You expand our capacity to wait on You. We ask that You increase our fortitude. Increase our ability to keep our eyes focused on You. Give us tunnel vision Father. Keep us solely focused on You and Your purpose for our lives. Help us to keep our eyes on our own tests Father. May we mind our business, and in the time of silence take advantage and prepare for our next assignment by exercising our spirits instead of feeding our flesh. May we always be willing vessels ready to be used for Your glorious servitude. We pray that You will empty us and free us from the bondage of our flesh and fill us to overflowing with Your benevolent spirit. Father we ask that You break up the fallow ground in us and annoint our spirits with the seed required to produce the Your fruit. Allow us to be plentiful with the fruits of love, peace, joy, goodness, graciousness, long suffering, temperance, mercy, gentleness, and meekness. Allow us to be walking examples of Your character. Allow us to walk in perfection just as You are truly perfect. We ask that You break the strongholds in our minds that keep us rebelling against Your order. We ask that You rebuild our minds, breaking down barriers and walls that have been built through adversity and disobedience. Restore us to You Father. Reclaim our minds and our thoughts. Bring us into submission of Your ways. Allow us to accept the rest that You offer us. Allow us to revel in the peace that you provide. Allow us to reap the benefits of being provided for by the ultimate provider. Father we ask that you release us from the bondage of mental and physical slavery that prevents us from accepting that we have been set free from every reason to have anxiety, worry, and fear. We rebuke every evil and wicked force that would attempt to rob us of our joy and peace. Every deceptive suggestion that would attempt to cause us to rise against your provision Father. Help us to stay in our place as your daughters. We ask that you send the Holy spirit to be a constant reminder of Your will for our life and we pray that Your will continue to be done in our lives. Let your kingdom come Father and let it begin in us. Let us walk in our positions as the bringers of life. Let us bring forth Your kingdom by Your hand let it be accomplished. By Your breath let it be manifested, in such a way that the earth will marvel at Your magnificence. We pray You get all the glory and honor. We stand in expectancy that all these things are being brought to last as we pray them for they are also Your desires. These things have already been written and it is done. So be it.

1 Peter 1:7 so that the proof of your faith, being more precious than gold which is perishable, even though tested by fire, may be found to result in praise and glory and honor at the revelation of Christ

Proverbs 3:11-12 My son, despise not the chastening of the Lord; neither be weary of his correction:12 For whom the Lord loveth he correcteth; even as a father the son in whom he delighteth.

Psalms 46:10 Be still, and know that I am God: I will be exalted among

the heathen, I will be exalted in the earth.

Matthew 5:48 Be ye therefore perfect, even as your Father which is in heaven is perfect

Hosea 10:12 Sow to yourselves in righteousness, reap in mercy; break up your fallow ground: for it is time to seek the Lord, till he come and rain righteousness upon you.

Galatians 5:22-23 But the fruit of the Spirit is love, joy, peace, longsuffering, gentleness, goodness, faith, Meekness, temperance: against such there is no law.

Romans 12:2 And be not conformed to this world: but be ye transformed by the renewing of your mind, that ye may prove what is that good, and acceptable, and perfect, will of God

2 Corinthians 10:4
(For the weapons of our warfare are not carnal, but mighty through God to the pulling down of strong holds;

Matthew 11:29-30 Take my yoke upon you, and learn of me; for I am meek and lowly in heart: and ye shall find rest unto your souls. For my yoke is easy, and my burden is light

DAY 5

Father we come before you in humility and reverence. We give you honor and glory for You alone are worthy to be praised. We ask for grace and mercy in our time of need Father. We ask for forgiveness and pardon Father for our disobedience. Grant us reprieve Father. You know us. You have searched our hearts, minds, and spirits and nothing can be hidden from you. You know our desires and the longings of our hearts Father. You know our comings and our goings. You understand our thoughts You know the path before us . You see our dreams and our fears Father. Nothing is outside of your knowledge. You know our strengths and our weaknesses. You know our habits and our talents Father. There is not a word I could speak that You don't know beforehand. You knew us in our darkness and saw fit to bring us into Your light. You have put Your hand on us. You have chosen us from among the millions of people You could have chosen and the knowledge of that is overwhelming . Your love for us is so high we cannot fully comprehend it. How could we ever leave You again when you have not forsaken us. Even in our disobedience You have kept us for Yourself. There is no place we could go that You aren't present. There is no problem or trial we have that you aren't aware of. No matter where we go or what we go through Your hand keeps us and You have promised that You hold us up with a your right hand. Even in the world full death and destruction Your light protects and surrounds us. The darkness cannot hide from You. All things bow to Your dominion. You created us and You have covered us from before our birth. We praise You; for we are fearfully and wonderfully made: marvellous are Your works. We are forever thankful that You are allowing us to learn Your righteousness . Surely You will slay the wicked on our behalf. For they move against You wickedly, and Your enemies take Your name in vain. Although it seems like it is us that the wickedness rises up against we know it isn't Wickedness rises against You Father. They attack Your spirit in us that they see. It is the goodness in us from Your love that wrestles against their wicked flesh. Your enemies are our enemies Father . We defend Your name just as You defend us Father and with You we know there is no need to fear. Your word says be not afraid nor dismayed by reason of this great multitude that comes against us for the battle is not ours, but Yours. We need not fight in this battle: set yourselves, stand still, and see the salvation of the Father with us. Fear not, nor be dismayed for the Most High will be with you. You are our protector and provider. Search us, Most High, and know our hearts, try us, and know our thoughts. And see if there be any wicked way in us, and lead us in the way everlasting. Cleanse us of every unrighteousness. Forge in us an unshakable faith and a mountain of patience. Renew in us the ability to trust You blindly. Forge in us the ability to endure u to salvation Father. We have nothing without You. We cannot save ourselves. We need Your strength and Your guidance. We need You to lead, guide, and direct our paths. We will not move without Your direction Father. Let Your hand continue to be upon us and Your words and Your praise be in our mouths at all times. We love You Father and we wait expectantly for You to show Your mighty hand in our lives. Thank You Father in advance. Its is written and it is done. So be it.

Jeremiah 17:10 I the Lord search the heart, I try the reins, even to give every man according to his ways, and according to the fruit of his doings.

Psalm 139 O lord, thou hast searched me, and known me. Thou knowest my downsitting and mine uprising, thou understandest my thought afar off.Thou compassest my path and my lying down, and art acquainted with all my ways.For there is not a word in my tongue, but, lo, O Lord, thou knowest it altogether.Thou hast beset me behind and before, and laid thine hand upon me.Such knowledge is too wonderful for me; it is high, I cannot attain unto it.Whither shall I go from thy spirit? or whither shall I flee from thy presence? If I ascend up into heaven, thou art there: if I make my bed in hell, behold, thou art there. If I take the

wings of the morning, and dwell in the uttermost parts of the sea;Even there shall thy hand lead me, and thy right hand shall hold me. If I say, Surely the darkness shall cover me; even the night shall be light about me. Yea, the darkness hideth not from thee; but the night shineth as the day: the darkness and the light are both alike to thee.For thou hast possessed my reins: thou hast covered me in my mother's womb. I will praise thee; for I am fearfully and wonderfully made: marvellous are thy works; and that my soul knoweth right well. My substance was not hid from thee, when I was made in secret, and curiously wrought in the lowest parts of the earth. Thine eyes did see my substance, yet being unperfect; and in thy book all my members were written, which in continuance were fashioned, when as yet there was none of them. How precious also are thy thoughts unto me, O God! how great is the sum of them! If I should count them, they are more in number than the sand: when I awake, I am still with thee. Surely thou wilt slay the wicked, O God: depart from me therefore, ye bloody men. For they speak against thee wickedly, and thine enemies take thy name in vain. Do not I hate them, O Lord, that hate thee? and am not I grieved with those that rise up against thee?I hate them with perfect hatred: I count them mine enemies.Search me, O God, and know my heart: try me, and know my thoughts:And see if there be any wicked way in me, and lead me in the way everlas

DAY 6

Father, Thank You, for Your amazing grace! We thank you for allowing us to receive Your grace – Your power, ability, and help – in every area of our lives to accomplish all that You desire for us to accomplish. Your grace strengthens us to stand no matter what comes our way. Your grace is sufficient for us. Assure us that Your grace and strength is all we need. Help us to be capable, intelligent, and virtuous women – faithful, diligent, generous and spiritually strong in

Your sight. May Your law of love and kindness always be in our hearts and on our lips. We determine to continually allow Your Word to dwell in us. As we grow in Your Word, help us to always be obedient to it, and to Your will in every area of our lives. We ask You to help us reflect Your love to each child we come in contact with. Help us to be the best examples of Your love and law that we can be. For the mothers allow us to raise them in Your tender nurture, training, discipline, counsel and admonition. For the aunts, sisters, cousins, allow us to influence them through our own righteousness. Help those of us who are married to be a loving and excellent wives to their husbands so that they will be able to trust confidently and unreservedly in their wives. May we as women, called to be the body, greatly enrich the lives of the appointed heads, comforting, encouraging and doing them good as long as there is life within us. We ask You for wisdom as we manage our homes. Help us to look well to how things are run, and refuse to eat the bread of idleness. Help us to avoid gossip, discontention or self-pity. Let us be gracious and grateful for the blessings and the trials. Show us how to organize our day and be more productive with our time always prioritizing and placing Your work as our priority. Father, we trust in You and keep our thoughts fixed on You and Your promises and You keep us in perfect peace. Let Your peace rule in our hearts. Allow it to settle any questions that arise in our minds, and to quell any doubtful thoughts that may arise. We wholeheartedly trust in You. Father, we thank You that You love us and that You care about everything that concerns us and our families. Today, we cast every care on You, knowing that You will take care of us. With Your help, we refuse to worry, or have any anxiety about anything. Instead, we thank You in advance for meeting all of our needs and working out every situation for Your glory. We trust in Your faithfulness.You know what we need and You will provide for our families, our nation and us. We determine to seek first Your Kingdom and Your righteousness, and we know that all the things we need will be given to us. You are always faithful to supply all our needs according to Your riches in glory by Christ. We come to you today to put on our armor and to stir up our dedication to You. Today we put on the helmet of salvation. We choose to rejoice in all the blessings that You have given us. We put on the belt of truth. Today we dedicate ourselves to Your truth. We honor your Word. We purpose to allow Your Word to guide us this day and every day. We put on the breastplate of righteousness.We dedicate ourselves to purity and righteous living. We put on the sandals of peace and dedicate ourselves to staying in perfect peace with You and walking in Your spirit. We take up the shield of faith and dedicate ourselves to growing in Faith and assurance of You. We take up the sword of the spirit which is Your word and dedicate ourselves to residing in your Word and using Your word in every aspect of our daily lives. Allow us to become more comfortable with speaking out about and standing on your Word. For we know the plans You have for us plans for good and not for evil, to give us a future and an expected end. Father, we trust You with all our hearts. We have full assurance that you have planned something bigger for our lives, something that we have always wanted. Bless us , Father, with patience that we will wait eagerly as You continue to unfold what you have planned for us. We pray that we be free from all forms of pride,vanity, ego , and lusts of the flesh. We believe that we are beautiful in Your eyes and Your judgment is the only thing that really matters. May we be free of our insecurities. Without them, we may be free and we may live in peace with our sister, brothers and ourselves. Father, we pray for every sister that may be secretly or even openly hurting and carrying heavy burdens, whether it be depression, doubt, anger, envy, hatred, unforgiveness, or any other grievous burden that rises up against the perfect peace You provide. You know our hearts and every detail of what we are going through. Even though we may not share every issue of what we are going through, or even share about our struggles and downfalls, we pray that You will meet us right where we are. We pray for opportunities to open up and share our struggles and our triumphs and allow our tests to be our testimonies and Your glorious praise reports. We also pray for discernment and sensitivity to not offend our sisters when they come to us in need. Help us to lean and let others lean on us while we wait on You to renew and restore every broken piece and refine every jewel. We thank you in advance for answering our prayers and meeting our needs. We thank you that our desires are granted because they are Your desires and will bring You all the glory You alone deserve. We believe that we receive it and we claim it. It is written so it is done. So be it.

2 Corinthians 12:9 And he said unto me, My grace is sufficient for thee: for my strength is made perfect in weakness. Most gladly therefore will I rather glory in my infirmities, that the power of Christ may rest upon me.

Malachi 2:6 The law of truth was in his mouth, and iniquity was not found in his lips: he walked with me in peace and equity, and did turn many away from iniquity.

1 Peter 5:7 Casting all your care upon him; for he careth for you

Philippians 4:19 But my God shall supply all your need according to his riches in glory by Christ Jesus.

Matthew 6:33 But seek ye first the kingdom of God, and his righteousness; and all these things shall be added unto you.

Jeremiah 29:11-13 For I know the thoughts that I think toward you, saith the Lord, thoughts of peace, and not of evil, to give you an expected end. Then shall ye call upon me, and ye shall go and pray unto me, and I will hearken unto you. And ye shall seek me, and find me, when ye shall search for me with all your heart

.

DAY 7

Heavenly Father we thank You for this day. Thank You for Your mercy Father. We thank You for all of Your provision, protection, and planning on our behalf. Thank You for not allowing us to reap the wages of sin, for Your redemption. Thank You for continuously keeping us even when we moan and groan in complaint instead of glorifying You in praise. Thank You for being the gracious and loving Father when we haven't loved You as we should. Forgive us for not living up to the standard You created us for. Forgive us for not having the reverence for Your holiness that we should. Forgive us for condemning each other without correcting ourselves. Forgive us for not walking in love. Forgive us for any unrighteous thing we have done that was displeasing in Your sight. Please continue to have mercy on us Father. Help us to walk in Your ways and to honor you with every thought, every step, every action we execute. Father teach us Your will. Show us what You would have us see through Your vision. Allow us to see each other through Your eyes. Allow us to see ourselves through Your eyes and to act accordingly. Show us to have faith in Your vision even when we can't see it. Expose us to Your thoughts Father for they are higher than ours. Grant us wisdom and understanding. Your ways are pure. Father, help us to trust Your direction and the plan You have for us over the plan we have for ourselves. Help us to keep our eyes focused on You no matter what happens in the left or the right of us. Prevent us from being shaken or moved. Keep our mouths full of praise and talk of Your glory. Keep us from glorifying the event with our flesh. Let us be walking billboards for your Majesty. Use us Father in the midst of our struggles, in spite of our trials. Empty us of every opposing thing, uproot the weeds that stifle the growth of the fruit you have ordained us to produce. Let us overflow with good fruit. Let our praise be a sweet sound in Your ears. Let our sacrifice of self be a sweet savor in Your nose Father. Let the work of our hands be governed by Your spirit and pleasing in Your sight. Fill us with your essence Father. You are the Potter, reshape us in your image, Father.

We cannot complete our mission without you. We are nothing without you. We cannot begin to become all You desire and deserve for us to be without You. Bless us with the ability to become worthy to serve in Your name Father; Righteous enough to sit at your feet. We long to please You Father teach us how. We long to hear"well done". We ask that You help us to stay focused on You and Your will. Do not let the cares of this life tear us away from You. Lift us above every obstacle that seeks to drown us in despair. Bless us with Your fire and give us zeal to complete Your works. Fill us with love and long suffering, realizing that Your work in each of Your children will be completed in Your timing and that Your work and Your timing are perfect. Let Your will be done in us and our lives Father. We ask for all these things knowing Your way is perfect, Your will is best, and Your love and strength is all we ever need. We ask on the premise that whatever we ask for we shall receive, because we believe. We ask for Your kingdom to come, Your will be done on earth and in our lives as it is in heaven. It is written and it is already done. So be it.

Romans 6:23 For the wages of sin is death; but the gift of God is eternal life through Jesus Christ our Lord.

John 15:16 Ye have not chosen me, but I have chosen you, and ordained you, that ye should go and bring forth fruit, and that your fruit should remain: that whatsoever ye shall ask of the Father in my name, he may give it you

Mark 4:19-20 And the cares of this world, and the deceitfulness of riches, and the lusts of other things entering in, choke the word, and it becometh unfruitful. And these are they which are sown on good ground; such as hear the word, and receive it, and bring forth fruit, some thirtyfold, some sixty, and some an hundred

DAY 8

Heavenly Father we come before You with praise and Thanksgiving. We thank You for this day, a day we did not have to live to see. Thank You for Your majesty. You alone are worthy of our praise. Holy is Your name. You are full of honor and there is none like You. Your Kingdom come and Your will be done in our lives and on earth as it is in heaven. We thank You Father for constantly and consistently providing for us. You meet our every need. Forgive us for every trespass we have committed against You Father. We thank You for the grace and mercy You give us even though we are undeserving. Help us to treat our brother and sisters with the same grace, mercy, and love that You give us so freely. Allow us to forgive as You forgive. To remember those things that have been done against us no more. We know vengeance and judgement is Yours Father. Teach us to leave those transgressions and those who transgress against us at Your feet. We pray that You extend your hand among us and bless us with Your character. Lead, guide, and direct us away from all wickedness. We pray the angels be encamped about and around us keeping us from even dashing our foot against a stone. Keep us from evil. Enlarge our territory Father. Enlarge our borders and the area that the light that shines through us reaches. Use us to be a beacon and a blessing near and far. Let your fruits overflow in us and onto those you send us to minister to. Gather us together Father. Allow us to be surrounded by Your spirit and Your righteousness. Allow us to be submersed in the truth. Let it cover our heads to our feet. May we walk in truth and follow the truth. May we seek the truth, alway speaking the truth. May we see the truth, and receive the truth. Father, You are our fortress. In You alone do we trust. You are our only help, our only source, our one true power. In you we have no want. You make it possible for us to lie down and sleep peacefully and protected. You hydrate us with living waters. You are the restored of our souls. You lead us in Your path of righteousness, and all the glory is Yours. Even though we walk through this world filled with the adversary, wickedness, and death, we have no fear. You are always with us, even until the ends of the earth. Your word, and Your spirit comfort us. You prepare a way for us out of no way and bless us with the abundance of our enemies. You anoint us with Your Holy Spirit who grants us wisdom, knowledge, and understanding. With you there is never lack. Surely Your goodness and mercy will abound in our lives for the rest of our life and if it be Your will we will abide with You in Your kingdom for eternity. We claim these things for they are written and already done. So be it.

Psalms 100:4 Enter into his gates with thanksgiving, and into his courts with praise: be thankful unto him, and bless his name.

Matthew 6:10 Thy kingdom come, Thy will be done in earth, as it is in heaven.

Psalm 91:11-12 For he shall give his angels charge over thee, to keep thee in all thy ways. They shall bear thee up in their hands, lest thou dash thy foot against a stone.

1 Chronicles 4:10 And Jabez called on the God of Israel, saying, Oh that thou wouldest bless me indeed, and enlarge my coast, and that thine hand might be with me, and that thou wouldest keep me from evil, that it may not grieve me! And God granted him that which he requested.

Psalms 91:2 I will say of the LORD, He is my refuge and my fortress: my God; in him will I trust.

John 16:13 Howbeit when he, the Spirit of truth, is come, he will guide you into all truth: for he shall not speak of himself; but whatsoever he shall hear, that shall he speak: and he will shew you things to come

Psalms 23:6 Surely goodness and mercy shall follow me all the days of my life: and I will dwell in the house of the LORD for ever.

DAY 9

Unto You, O Most High, do we lift up our souls. We trust in you: let us not be ashamed, let not our enemies triumph over us. Save us from the shame of defeat; don't let our enemies gloat over us!Your word says none that wait on You will be ashamed: let them be ashamed those who do unrighteousness without cause. Defeat does

not come to those who trust in you, but to those who are quick to rebel against you.Show us Your ways, Father; teach us Your paths. Teach us to live according to your truth for you are our God, who saves us. Lead us in Your truth, and teach us: for You are the God of our salvation; on thee do we wait all day. We always trust in you. Remember, O Most High, Your tender mercies and thy loving kindnesses; for they have been ever of old.

Remember not the sins of our youth, nor our transgressions: according to thy mercy remember us for Your goodness' sake.In your constant love and goodness, remember us Father . Because you are righteous and good. Holy and upright is the Most High: therefore will You teach sinners in Your way. You guide the meek in judgment: You lead the humble in the right way and teach them Your will. With faithfulness and love you lead all who keep your covenant and obey your commands. All the paths of the Most High are mercy and truth unto those that keep his covenant and his

testimonies.For Your name's sake pardon our iniquity; for it is great. What man is he that feareth the Lord? him shall The Most High teach in the way that He shall choose. His soul shall dwell at ease; and his seed shall inherit the earth. They will always be prosperous, and their children will possess the land. The secret of the Father is with them that fear him; and he will shew them

his covenant. Our eyes are ever looking toward You; for You alone shall pluck our feet out of the net. Turn thee unto us, and have mercy upon us; for we are desolate and afflicted.The troubles of our hearts are enlarged: bring us out of our distresses. Look upon our affliction and our pain; and forgive all of our sins. Be merciful to us, because we are lonely and weak.Relieve us of our worries and save us from all our troubles. Consider our distress and suffering and forgive all our sins. Consider our enemies; for they are many; they hate us with cruel hatred. O keep our soul, and deliver us: let us not be ashamed; for we put our trust in thee. Let integrity and uprightness preserve us for we wait on thee. Redeem Israel, O Most High God out of all its troubles. Selah

Psalm 25
Unto thee, O Lord, do I lift up my soul. O my God, I trust in thee: let me not be ashamed, let not mine enemies triumph over me. Yea, let none that wait on thee be ashamed: let them be ashamed which transgress without cause. Shew me thy ways, O Lord; teach me thy paths. Lead me in thy truth, and teach me: for thou art the God of my salvation; on thee do I wait all the day.Remember, O Lord, thy tender mercies and thy lovingkindnesses; for they have been ever of old.Remember not the sins of my youth, nor my transgressions: according to thy mercy remember thou me for thy goodness' sake, O Lord.Good and upright is the Lord: therefore will he teach sinners in the way.The meek will he guide in judgment: and the meek will he teach his way.All the paths of the Lord are mercy and truth unto such as keep his covenant and his testimonies.For thy name's sake, O Lord, pardon mine iniquity; for it is great.What man is he that feareth the Lord? him shall he teach in the way that he shall choose. His soul shall dwell at ease; and his seed shall inherit the earth.The secret of the Lord is with them that fear him; and he will shew them his covenant.Mine eyes are ever toward the Lord; for he shall pluck my feet out of the net. Turn thee unto me, and have mercy upon me; for I am desolate and afflicted. The troubles of my heart are enlarged: O bring thou me out of my distresses. Look upon mine affliction and my pain; and forgive all my sins.Consider mine enemies; for they are many; and they hate me with cruel hatred. O keep my soul, and deliver me: let me not be ashamed; for I put my trust in thee.Let integrity and uprightness preserve me; for I wait on thee.Redeem Israel, O God, out of all his troubles.

Day 10

Father we thank You for the ability to come to You as a whole. We thank You for every blessing big and small, the trials and the resting times. Thank You for the things that seem like hardship that are for our own good. The things that have been set up to grow our faith and patience . Thank You for exercising our endurance. Thank You for all You give us and do for us. Thank You for providing for us the things we need that we don't even know we need. Thank You for the things You provide for our benefit, and for the protection You give us. Even the protection You give us from ourselves. We give You all the glory. Please forgive us for displeasing You in any way. Thank You for the grace and mercy You provide us through Your forgiveness. We pray to do better today than we did yesterday constantly working towards the perfection You created us for. Father, we ask that your will be done in our lives. That you order and guide our steps and that when your timing is manifested and it's time for us to move let us have assuredness in the directions you give us. Make it crystal clear Father which way you will have us to go. Protect us from the spirit of doubt and distrust that would seek to intervene in Your plan for our life. Protect us from the strongholds that cause us to hesitate when you say move. Protect us from any unrighteous advice. Protect us from thinking ourselves out of the blessings you have ordained for us. Protect us from the enemy that longs to cheat us out of our inheritance and our place in Your kingdom. Let Your will be sovereign in our lives. We long to obey you and many times we are unsure if we hear your voice because of the outside interference sent for this exact reason, to confuse us. Our spirits long to walk in Your way but many times we are hesitant that the path we think we are being led down is Your specific path for our lives. We ask that you guard our ears from the adversary voices. Let your voice be loud and sure in our spirits. We ask the Holy Spirit to be with us and guide us towards or away from the path we should walk. Order our steps. And when unassuredness still exists because of the strongholds of our minds and the deceptions of this world please send us confirmations that will solidify Your direction in our sight. Give us assuredness in our steps. We pray against fear and bind any spirit of anxiety, apprehension, doubt, panic, distress, agitation of the spirit that may come against us when moving in Your will. Bless us with the spirit of peace, strength, confidence, and most of all faith in you and your decision for our life. Build in us the faith to step out. To walk in the faith of Your word that said you will never leave us or forsake us. Please do not allow us to be hampered by the accusations and darts the enemy attempts to throw at us that say we have disobeyed and are no longer in your will. Allow us to walk in the forgiveness that you have blessed us with through your grace and mercy and through no deserving of our own. Allow us to accept the loving kindness you provide. Father we pray against the strongholds that seek to keep us separated. Join us together Father. Allow us to unite in love and obedience and with the objective to please you. We pray against the strongholds that have been erected in our minds that cause us to suspect or be untrusting. We know that in You alone should we place our trust. Keep us from allowing the doubt that has grown from trusting man to cloud and prevent us from putting our trust in You where it belongs. You are the only one we can trust. You alone are the honorable and good one in this earth. Let us be assured that placing our trust in you is safety. We ask that you tear down the stronghold of our thoughts. Renew our minds to think your thoughts, renew our hearts to not love hesitantly. Give us comfort in the fruits of the spirit. Rebuke our flesh and crucify it. We pray against this flesh that would attempt to constantly remind us of our past mistakes and pain to keep us in bondage to those things. Trusting You will never lend the same results as trusting in the world. Loving in the kingdom will never feel like what we have been convinced that love was in this wicked system. Keep us mindful of that as we walk with You and in Your way. We ask all of these things for Your glory and the progression of Your kingdom. We wait in expectancy of an answer in affirmation of these prayers. We pray above all that Your will be done. We thank You in advance. So be it.

Psalms 119:133 Order my steps in thy word: and let not any iniquity have dominion over me

1 Corinthians 10:13 There hath no temptation taken you but such as is common to man: but God is faithful, who will not suffer you to be tempted above that ye are able; but will with the temptation also make a way to escape, that ye may be able to bear it.

Romans 12:2 And be not conformed to this world: but be ye transformed

by the renewing of your mind, that ye may prove what is that good, and acceptable, and perfect, will of God

DAY 11

Oh heavenly Father Holy is your name. Your kingdom come Your will be done in our lives as it is in Heaven. We thank you for blessing in this and every day with provisions of every type. You bless us not only with physical food but also with living water. You feed our spirits Father. Forgive us of our sins and every unrighteous act we have committed that has displeased you Father. Have grace and mercy on us and allow us to have that same grace and mercy for those who sin against us. Lead us and guide us Father. We pray that you keep us from all evil and wickedness. Provide us a way out of every temptation. Lord, may nothing separate us from You today. Teach us how to submit to Your way today. Order our steps so that each step will lead us closer to Your will. Help us to resist walking in our emotions but to walk by the truth which is Your Word. Keep our hearts pure and undivided. Protect us from any careless , vain, or prideful thoughts, words, and actions. Prevent us from being distracted by flesh. Help us to distinguish between our wants, desires, and thoughts on how our lives should be and Yours. Help us to embrace each obstacle that comes our way as an opportunity for growth... Instead of a personal inconvenience. You already know the ways we will fall short and mess up. But we recognize Your love for us is not based on our performance. You love us flaws and all and have since before we were born. You have claimed us for your own and continuously mold us into who you have created us to be. And in our day of trouble we will call on You knowing that You will answer us and You will save us. For you are our protection, our fortress, and only in You will we trust. Among the gods there is none like You, Father; neither are there any works like Your work. You are great, and do wondrous things: You are the Most High alone. Teach us Your ways and we will walk in Your truth: teach our hearts to fear Your name. We will praise You Father, with all of our hearts: and we will glorify Your name forever. Give us strength in our weakness. Give us faith in place of our fear. Give us power in place of our powerlessness. For great is Your mercy toward us: and only You can deliver our souls from the lowest hell. When we are tempted to give up, give us the motivation to keep going. Grant us a cheerful spirit when adversity comes our way. And give us courage to accomplish whatever task you set before us. Let us not back down because of doubt or fear. Because You have not given us a spirit of fear but of love, joy, power, and a sound mind. Often our hearts are heavy. We are surrounded by loneliness and despair and it seems like we have to carry the burden alone. Words like overwhelmed, distraught, exhausted seem to describe our thoughts many times. And sometimes Father we are not exactly sure of how to let you carry the heavy load. Please show us how to release the burdens that do not belong to us. Show us how to be obedient and allow you to have full and complete control. Take these burdens from us. Let us find complete rest and be refreshed so that our heart won't be heavy. We know that these, our prayers are Your desires. That we desire what will give You the glory. We ask for these things in assurance and expectancy. We thank You in advance that You are granting each request and that through them and much more You will be glorified. We claim these things in Your power and might for they have been written and are already done in the spirit soon to be manifested in the flesh. So be it.

Psalm 86 Bow down thine ear, O Lord, hear me: for I am poor and needy.Preserve my soul; for I am holy: O thou my God, save thy servant that trusteth in thee. Be merciful unto me, O Lord: for I cry unto thee daily.Rejoice the soul of thy servant: for unto thee, O Lord, do I lift up my soul. For thou, Lord, art good, and ready to forgive; and plenteous in mercy unto all them that call upon thee. Give ear, O Lord, unto my prayer; and attend to the voice of my supplications. In the day of my trouble I will call upon thee: for thou wilt answer me.Among the gods there is none like unto thee, O Lord; neither are there any works like unto thy works. All nations whom thou hast made shall come and worship before thee, O Lord; and shall glorify thy name. For thou art great, and doest wondrous things: thou art God alone. Teach me thy way, O Lord; I will walk in thy truth: unite my heart to fear thy name. I will praise thee, O Lord my God, with all my heart: and I will glorify thy name for evermore.For great is thy mercy toward me: and thou hast delivered my soul from the lowest hell. O God, the proud are risen against me, and the assemblies of violent men have sought after my soul; and have not set thee before them. But thou, O Lord, art a God full of

compassion, and gracious, long suffering, and plenteous in mercy and truth.O turn unto me, and have mercy upon me; give thy strength unto thy servant, and save the son of thine handmaid.Shew me a token for good; that they which hate me may see it, and be ashamed: because thou, Lord, hast holpen me, and comforted me.

Psalm 91:2 I will say of the Lord, He is my refuge and my fortress: my God; in him will I trust.

Day 12

Heavenly Father we come to you in our weakness. We come with thankfulness that we have the ability to come before You. You are our shelter, and our fortress. In You do we trust. Please forgive us for anything we have done that was displeasing in Your sight. Forgive us for any words spoken, any thoughts, or actions that may have unknowingly separated us from pleasing You. Purge us Father and cleanse us. Make us pleasing in Your sight. Have mercy on us Father. Cover us in Your grace please. We have such a strong need for you daily. There is no way we can make it through these days living in this wicked world without You Father. But we desire to please you. We desire to accomplish the tasks set before us and meet Your expectations. Yet we are weary. We feel the weight of the wickedness surrounding us daily. Your word says You will sustain us, that if we cry out You will hear us and rescue us. So please hear our cries Father. Your word says that it is through our weakness that we will be made strong. So we fall before you, pleading for mercy and strength to endure through these hard times. Please give us the strength to stand when our families, friends, and people we love turn their backs on us. Make us stronger when the longings of our flesh desire to be filled. Hold us up when our flesh rises up against us and we begin to miss the illusions of love we once had, the illusions of happiness, and the lusts of the flesh. Give us the strength to continue to believe, and have faith when all we see is what looks like our failure, when it seems like everything is turning against us and nothing is in our favor. For Your word says that with You for us who could be against us Father. Your word says that victory is in You and that Your children will be the head and not the tail, above and not beneath, the blessings of Abraham are promised to us. Keep this on our minds in spite of what our fleshly eyes see. Help us to have blind faith. Please do not allow this evil world and the unrighteousness we have to endure cause us to harden our hearts. Hold us in your unchanging hand Father and let nothing pluck us from it. We plead for you to rescue us. Show Yourself mighty in the face of our adversity Father. We need You. Many days the attacks seem to be too much and the weight too heavy to bear. But Your word says if we seek You first and your kingdom everything will be added unto us. That if we trust in You You will provide, protect, and defend us. Avenge us Father from those who prey on us because we seek to please You and do Your will. To the world we are the weak. Rise us up Father in Your power and show them that righteousness isn't weakness but strength. They have no idea how hard this walk is. Lighten our loads Father. Take our burdens and give us peace that passes all understanding that will continue to keep our hearts and minds stayed on obeying you. Don't let us get distracted by pain and sorrow Father. Don't let thoughts of depression and solitude take us down into the pits that the enemy has dug for our downfall. Your word says that you will provide us a way out of every temptation. Many days we are tempted to quit Father. Many days we are tempted to give in to the fleshly responses that constantly rise up when confronted with other's fleshly behaviors. We are often tempted, Father. Temptation is tiring. Provide us with a way out of the stress and strain Father. As we continue to endure, renew our strength. Rise us up above the fleshly distractions sent against us everyday. Let us mount up on Your wings like the eagles. Help us to succeed so You will get all of the glory. Don't let us fall Father. We ask all these things in Your might and power. We ask because these things will allow us to accomplish the goals You have set before us. We ask because these things will bring You glory before the nations, Father. We ask according to Your will. Let it be done in the flesh as it is already in the spirit. It is written and it is done. So be it.

Psalms 34:17 The righteous cry, and the LORD heareth, and delivereth

them out of all their troubles.

2 Corinthians 12:9-10 And he said unto me, My grace is sufficient for thee: for my strength is made perfect in weakness. Most gladly therefore will I rather glory in my infirmities, that the power of Christ may rest upon me. Therefore I take pleasure in infirmities, in reproaches, in necessities, in persecutions, in distresses for Christ's sake: for when I am weak, then am I strong.

Romans 8:31 What shall we then say to these things? If God be for us, who can be against us?

Deuteronomy 28:13And the Lord shall make thee the head, and not the tail; and thou shalt be above only, and thou shalt not be beneath; if that thou hearken unto the commandments of the Lord thy God, which I command thee this day, to observe and to do them.

Philippians 4:7 And the peace of God, which passeth all understanding, shall keep your hearts and minds through Christ Jesus.

Isaiah 40:31But they that wait upon the LORD shall renew their strength; they shall mount up with wings as eagles; they shall run, and not be weary; and they shall walk, and not faint.

Day 13

Heavenly Father we come to You with praise and worship in our mouths. We honor you Father for You alone are worthy to be praised. We ask for forgiveness for any and everything we have done to displease you knowingly or unknowingly. Please have mercy on us Father. Cover us with you grace and loving kindness. We ask for forgiveness on behalf of our forefathers. We ask forgiveness on behalf of our fallen counterparts. We call the missing portions into submission of Your will. We desire to obey You Father. We long to walk in Your ways and to do Your will. We ask that You order our steps. Cover us in Your Holy spirit to lead, guide, and direct us. Order our steps. Let our thoughts be Your thoughts. Let our ways be Your ways. Let us be what and who you created us to be. Father have Your way with us and in us. Have Your way in our lives. We submit to You Father. We submit our bodies to You as a living sacrifice. We submit our lives to You. We submit our wills to Your will. We acknowledge that without You we are nothing. We acknowledge that without you nothing is possible. We have no life outside of You Father. We submit to You through these storms. In the midst of the trials and tribulations Father we still honor You. We still desire Your will to be done, not our own. We pray that Your kingdom come and Your will be done. Let us lean not to our own understanding. Here we are Father seeking Your kingdom first, seeking Your will. We stand in faith that every need is met and every desire granted. That every piece and portion will be added unto us in Your perfect timing. We thank You that in You we have life for there is no death. Let light go before us and show us the way in everything we do. We thank You for the way that You make out of no way. We thank You that nothing is impossible to you and in our lives you make the impossible possible on our behalf. Thank you Father that even when it seems like there is no way out You are the way out. We thank you for this truth and calling us to walk in it. We thank You for your chastisement and the trials which you give to produce patience in us so that we may be able to endure. Thank You for growing our endurance Father for the time ahead. Thank You for loving us enough to prepare us. Thank You for protecting us not only from this wicked world but ourselves. Thank You for keeping us when we are ready to quit . For sending us reminders and righteous influences to send words of encouragement when our faith is failing. Thank You for our sisters and brothers. For the family to those with no family. For the smiles and joy in the midst of the storm. Thank You for the provision, protection, and Providence that You have prepared for us. You are such an awesome Father and we love You. Thank You for showing us true love. We thank You and we can't thank You enough Father. We ask these things in Your Holy name the Great I Am O Holy God of Israel the ONLY good in all creation. We all according to Your will and word. Because these are Your promises and You hasten to perform them. We wait on You in expectancy. For it is written and already done in the spirit now manifesting in the flesh. So be it.

Proverbs 3:5-6 Trust in the Lord with all thine heart; and lean not unto thine own understanding. In all thy ways acknowledge him, and he shall

direct thy paths.

Proverbs 12:28 In the way of righteousness is life; and in the pathway thereof there is no death.
Luke 1:37 For with God nothing shall be impossible.

Luke 18:19 And Jesus said unto him, Why callest thou me good? none is good, save one, that is, God.

Jeremiah 1:12 Then said the LORD unto me, Thou hast well seen: for I will hasten my word to perform it.

Day 14

Father we come before you today with praise and thanksgiving on our lips. Forgive us Father of our sins and trespasses against you. Forgive our heads and our forefathers as well. We pray Your mercy and grace continue to cover us. We glorify Your name Father. You alone are worthy of all the praises. Your law is perfect, converting the soul. Your testimony is sure, making wise the simple. Your statutes are right, rejoicing the heart: Your commandment is pure, enlightening the eyes. The fear of You is clean, enduring forever: Your judgments are true and righteous altogether. More to be desired are they than gold, sweeter also than honey and the honeycomb. By Your laws, statutes and judgements are Your servants warned: and in keeping of them there is great reward. Who can understand his errors? cleanse us from our secret faults. Keep back Your servants also from presumptuous sins; let them not have dominion over us: then we will be upright, and we shall be innocent from the great transgression. Let the words of our mouths, and the meditation of our hearts, be acceptable in Your sight, O Most High, our strength, and our redeemer. Your word says we will be like a tree planted by the rivers of water, that bringeth forth Your fruit in Your season; our leaf will not wither; and whatsoever we do will prosper. There are many that say of our souls there is no help for us in You. But You, O Great Most High God, are a shield for us ; our glory, and the lifter up of our heads. You are our rock, and our fortress, and our deliverer; our Power, our strength, in whom we will trust; our buckler, and the horn of our salvation, and our high tower. Hear us when we call, Father of our righteousness: You have caused us to grow as a result of being tried through trials; have mercy upon us and hear our prayer. We know that You have set apart him that is godly for Yourself. Your word says You will hear when we call You. We offer ourselves as sacrifices of righteousness, and put our trust in You. There are many that say that nothing good will come to us from obeying Your law. But we know the truth. Father, lift up the light of Your spirit and make it shine on us. Let all those that put their trust in You rejoice: let them ever shout for joy, because You defend us: let them also that love Your name be joyful in You. Because You will bless the righteous; with favour will You protect us and cover us. We thank You for Your covering. We thank You for Your will being done in our lives. We thank You that as we continue to trust You, You will continue to provide, protect, and bring to past the Providence you set for us before our births. Continue to lead, guide and direct us. Order our steps and keep us in the way of Your righteousness. We ask all these things in Your power and might. We pray that Your will be done in all and through all above our own wills. We submit our wills to You. We thank You in advance that what we ask has already been manifested in the spirit and will soon be manifested in the flesh. For we know what is loosed on earth is loosed already in heaven. Therefore we claim it and wait in expectancy for You to perform it. So be it.

Psalm 19:7-14 The law of the Lord is perfect, converting the soul: the

testimony of the Lord is sure, making wise the simple. The statutes of the Lord are right, rejoicing the heart: the commandment of the Lord is pure, enlightening the eyes. The fear of the Lord is clean, enduring for ever: the judgments of the Lord are true and righteous altogether. More to be desired are they than gold, yea, than much fine gold: sweeter also than honey and the honeycomb. Moreover by them is thy servant warned: and in keeping of them there is great reward. Who can understand his errors? cleanse thou me from secret faults. Keep back thy servant also from presumptuous sins; let them not have dominion over me: then shall I be upright, and I shall be innocent from the great transgression. Let the words of my mouth, and the meditation of my heart, be acceptable in thy sight, O Lord, my strength, and my redeemer.

Psalm 1:3 And he shall be like a tree planted by the rivers of water, that bringeth forth his fruit in his season; his leaf also shall not wither; and whatsoever he doeth shall prosper.

Psalms 5:11-12 But let all those that put their trust in thee rejoice: let them ever shout for joy, because thou defendest them: let them also that love thy name be joyful in thee.For thou, Lord, wilt bless the righteous; with favour wilt thou compass him as with a shield.

Day 15

Father we come before You thanking You for another day. Forgive us Father for any unrighteousness we have thought, believed, spoken, or acted on that is against Your will and has displeased you knowingly or unknowingly. We ask for forgiveness on behalf of our forefathers. We ask for forgiveness on behalf of not yet awakened Israel. We ask for forgiveness on behalf of our other halves, our heads, the righteous leaders of this nation. Have mercy on us all Father. We long to fulfill our destiny in your will Father. Your word says that before our births you knew us. You chose us to fulfill the destiny of producing fruit. You created us with this destiny in mind, gave us the ability to complete the mission, and have personally directed us and molded us into those that will be able to be successful at the tasks placed before us. We are eager to serve You Father. But sometimes we fail to see that in serving You we have to stop serving ourselves. We have to stop wanting our own way. We get in our own way, and even Your way Father. Forgive us. Because we are so grateful. When we take the time to consider what being chosen by you means Father we are overwhelmed,never wanting to disappoint You. We have been made with this specific purpose in mind. For this specific moment. For this specific testing period. There is NOTHING that is happening outside of Your will. You are in complete control. We submit ourselves willingly to You. Have Your way in our lives Father. We thank you for the storms Father. Thank you for the toughening. Thank you for the lessons Father. Thank you for taking the time to carefully plan and orchestrate each moment of our lives, providing each and every need, protecting us from each hidden disaster, proving us with each difficult test. We thank You for each and every opportunity to get in line with Your will. For each moment of grace and mercy that You have for us every time we let You down. Thank You Father for this chance to be used by You. We thank You Father for the opportunity to serve in Your kingdom. We thank You for choosing us as vessels for Your work. Thank You Father for emptying us of every impurity. For cleansing us of all unrighteousness. For trying us and purifying us as pure gold. For turning us from filth and wickedness into Your golden vessels. A golden vessel to be cleansed inside and out. A golden vessel to be presented before You without blemish.A golden vessel created by You and filled by you with life and the light of truth. To be used by You as a vessel to carry Your word which is life to others Father. We thank You for this opportunity. We know You could have chosen ANYBODY... but You chose us. Thank You for seeing in us what we could not see in ourselves. For seeing in us what others could not see. For placing in us a light that will shine so brightly that You will use it to draw all men unto You. A light that will shine so brightly others will fall before You and praise Your holy name. Thank You Father for Your truth. Thank You for the peace that passes all understanding. Thank You for the Holy Spirit which leads, guides, and directs us. Thank You for the fellowship that confirms the words of the Holy Spirit. Thank You for these bonds that You are forging. For fitting us together as one body moving in perfect unison, on one accord. We only say thank You Father because everything has already been asked for and every need has already been met. Every task has been accomplished in the spirit and is Now manifesting in the flesh. We call those things which be not as though they were because we expect for them to be so. Your word says it and we know You are not a man that You would lie and that You stand by Your word and hasten to perform it. We give you all the glory and all the praise. So be it.

Jeremiah 1:5
Before I formed thee in the belly I knew thee; and before thou camest forth out of the womb I sanctified thee, and I ordained thee a prophet unto the nations.

John 15:16 Ye have not chosen me, but I have chosen you, and ordained you, that ye should go and bring forth fruit, and that your fruit should remain: that whatsoever ye shall ask of the Father in my name, he may give it you.

1 John 1:9 If we confess our sins, he is faithful and just to forgive us our sins, and to cleanse us from all unrighteousness.

John 12:32 And I, if I be lifted up from the earth, will draw all men unto me.

John 16:13 Howbeit when he, the Spirit of truth, is come, he will guide you into all truth: for he shall not speak of himself; but whatsoever he shall hear, that shall he speak: and he will shew you things to come.

1 Corinthians 12:12 For as the body is one, and hath many members, and all the members of that one body, being many, are one body: so also is Christ.

Day 16

Heavenly Father we come to You in reverence. We bow before Your throne. We ask for forgiveness for anything we may have done that displeased You. We ask forgiveness on behalf of our ancestors and our heads. Have mercy on us. We thank you for bringing us to and through another day. We thank you for your guidance. We ask for peace in the midst of the storms Father. Give us assurance in our times of doubt. We thank You for these storms that are created to increase our faith in You Father. Build us up when the storms are beating us down. Bless us with Your supernatural strength when we get weary. Your word says we will walk and not be weary, we shall run and not faint. If we wait on you Father. We are waiting on you to renew our strength. To keep us standing in the face of adversity. We are waiting on you to show yourself mighty on our behalf Father. We stand in expectancy because we know these battles are beyond us. And that nothing is in our control. But You alone control all things. We know that for us alone these battles are impossible to overcome. But with you all things are possible. We thank you Father for choosing us to execute Your will. Thank You for the opportunity to be used by You. Thank you for your spirit of truth that leads us into all wisdom, knowledge and understanding. And when we lack understanding Father, remind us to not lean unto our own but in all of our ways to continue to acknowledge You and You will direct our paths. Continue to lead us in the path of righteousness for Your name's sake. That Your glory be proclaimed in all the earth. That Your goodness be known throughout every land Father. Just let us be the vessels Father. We thank you for the virtues that are growing in us. Thank you for the patience, and temperance, joy, and long suffering, peace, and goodness, meekness, and kindness and most of all love. We are honored to be examples of virtuous women in all of the earth. That through our behavior we will set the standard. No longer will wickedness be the norm but righteousness and modesty. That we will teach our daughters the virtues of our mother wisdom. We thank you that we are paving the way for the future generations to not have to suffer our walk. They will grow up in obedience, learning to walk in Your statues, laws , and commandments. They will love the law. They will not have to be purged. Let us continue to strive to be righteous examples to all who are watching us and attempting to learn through us. Allow us to be our sisters keepers. To love them righteously and offer our assistance to each other where needed. Allow us to support each other in our growth and constantly work towards the betterment of ourselves and the kingdom. Help us everyday to be better mothers, wives, and sisters and allow others to be the same for us in return. Remind us constantly of the grace and mercy we have received and keep us walking and giving the same. Guide us in our discernment and help us to honor You in our every endeavor. Let us glorify You is every word that proceeds from our mouths and every action that is performed without bodies. Let us conduct ourselves as the apple of Your eye and never bring You to shame. We long to please You Father. Thank You for allowing us a new opportunity to do so everyday. Let our today be better than our yesterday and our tomorrow be even better still. Until we be perfected and finally the manifestation of Your image in the flesh. We thank You for all you have done, all you are doing and all that is to come. We thank You in advance for the manifestation of our every need and desire being met and granted. We wait on You with expectancy. We claim the victory for it is already done. So be it.

Isaiah 40:31But they that wait upon the LORD shall renew their strength; they shall mount up with wings as eagles; they shall run, and not be weary; and they shall walk, and not faint.

Psalms 23:3 He restoreth my soul: he leadeth me in the paths of righteousness for his name's sake.

Psalms 19:14 Let the words of my mouth, and the meditation of my heart, be acceptable in thy sight, O LORD, my strength, and my

redeemer

Day 17

Father we come humbly before Your throne with praise and worship in our moths and Thanksgiving in our hearts. We ask for forgiveness for any unrighteous thoughts or actions we have committed against you. We ask for forgiveness on behalf of our ancestors and our heads. Have mercy on us Father. Please continue to grant us the opportunity to be made perfect in You. We pray on behalf of our sisterhood Father. We pray that for the rest of our lives—in whatever calling—we be completely devoted to Your glory. We commit that the promises of Your word be trusted so fully that peace and joy and strength fill our souls to overflowing. We ask that this fullness that belongs to only You Father, overflow in daily acts of love so that people might see Your goodness at work in us and give glory to You. We pledge that each of us be women of the Book, who love and study and obey the Bible in every area of its teaching; that meditation on biblical truth be the source of hope and faith; that we continue to grow in understanding through all the chapters of our lives. Let us always be women of prayer, so that Your Word will be made clear to us, and so the power of faith, perfect understanding and knowledge will descend upon us; that our spiritual influence may increase at home and wherever else You see fit to use us Father. We ask that you enlarge our understanding and that we innately connected with the Holy spirit and partake in her wisdom causing us to become deep thinkers about the doctrines of grace, and even deeper lovers of all things pertaining to righteousness and holiness. We long to be completely committed to ministry, whatever our specific calling may be; that we not be wasteful of our time but that we always keep Your work and Your Kingdom first in our lives. We pray that our single sisters use and dedicate their singleness to the full in devotion to Your work (the way Messiah and Paul did) and not be paralyzed or over run by the desire to be married. And likewise that, if the sister be married, we pray that they humbly, wisely and sincerely support the leadership of their husband, redirecting him as the head and Your representative; that You encourage him in his appointed role as head; that You constantly influence him spiritually, ordering his home, his steps, and their lives as one. We pray for the sisters with children, to accept responsibility to raise them up in the discipline and and righteous instruction of the Most High—children who hope in the triumph of His kingdom— teaching Your ways, and giving them the special attention they need from us as well as that loving them with the love we have been taught is real love, the love of our Father. Father please do not allow us to get so wrapped up in worldly matters that we begin to assume that worldly employment is a better provider or a better use of our lives than the countless opportunities of service and witness in the home, the neighborhood, the community, the church, and the world. Let us be willing vessels that You use at Your will in whatever way You see fit. We pray that You develop in us a wartime mentality and lifestyle; causes us to stay in constant remembrance that this is a war and everyday lives are lost, that billions of people hang in the balance of heaven and hell, that the love of money is is the root of all evil, that the lusts of the flesh are enmity with You, and that the thirst for material gain is a distraction and dangerous substitute for the goals of living for You with all that we are. We ask all these things for Your glory and for the progress of the kingdom that is coming. We ask above all we could ever pray that Your will be done in all and above all. We thank You for all You have done, all Your are doing, and all that is yet to come. We love You Father and we claim all that You have promised us and stand in expectancy of its manifestation in the flesh in Your perfect timing. Thank You for Your provision and protection and most of all Your providence. So be it.

1 Corinthians 7:8-10 I say therefore to the unmarried and widows, it is good for them if they abide even as I. But if they cannot contain, let them marry: for it is better to marry than to burn. And unto the married I command, yet not I, but the Lord, Let not the wife depart from her husband:

Colossians 3:2 - Set your affection on things above, not on things on the earth.
1 Timothy 6:10 For the love of money is the root of all evil: which while some coveted after, they have erred from the faith, and pierced themselves through with many sorrows.

Romans 8:5-8 For they that are after the flesh do mind the things of the flesh; but they that are after the Spirit the things of the Spirit.For to be carnally minded is death; but to be spiritually minded is life and peace.Because the carnal mind is enmity against God: for it is not subject to the law of God, neither indeed can be.So then they that are in the flesh cannot please God.

Day 18

Father we come to You in thanksgiving. First we ask for forgiveness for all we have thought, said, and done that was against You and Your will. We long to please you. Please forgive us on behalf of our ancestors and give that same forgiveness to our heads, the leaders of our nation. Have grace and mercy on us Father. Open our eyes to how we continue to sin against You. Send the Holy spirit to quicken us when we transgress against You. Please teach us to abide in Your ways. To speak only Your words and do only Your will. We praise you! From the depths of our hearts with all that we are , we praise Your holy name. You are the giver of all good gifts, and Your blessings are overwhelming. Thank You Father, for all You have done! The gift of Your Son, grace, and forgiveness have all come from Your generous and loving hand; and yet You have continued to pour out even more! Thank You for the gift of Your Word, which sustains and strengthens our faith. Thank You for always listening to and answering our prayers with your great wisdom and understanding.   Thank you for purchasing us with a price Father. That we are no longer our own. Thank you for your precious spirit sent to earth in the form of Our Messiah. For our redemption back to you even though we don't deserve it.   Thank You for choosing us to be Your daughters. You have filled our hearts with Your love and kindness; let us reflect that grace to others. You bring such contentment as we dwell on your mercy and love; and our hearts are encouraged as we are reminded of Your faithfulness. I praise You Father. We cannot thank You enough for all that You have done and continue to do for us. Purify our minds Father. Transform our thoughts by the power of Your Word. Show us where and when our thoughts about all things do not agree with Your thoughts. We need Your help to guard our hearts against bitterness, selfishness, and the temptation to pursue the attention of others. Guard us against the spirit of selfishness, envy, greed, lust, division, hatred, malice, idolatry, witchcraft, deceit, and vanity. Be our gentle shepherd. Lead us away from the activities and relationships that would keep me from prioritizing our relationship over every other earthly relationship. Increase in us the fruit of the spirit. We ask that you would empty us of every unclean thing Father. Empty us of ourselves and fill us to overflowing with You and all that You are. Help us to see ourselves as You see us. We long to align our thoughts with Your thoughts about us so that we become the woman, sister, mother, and wife You designed us to be. Let our ways be Your ways Father. Let our desires be the desires of Your heart. Let our hands move to Your work first. Let our feet never stray from Your path. Break down the walls of fear and pride that keep us from knowing who we became when we fully submitted our lives to Your will and You way. Have Your way in us Father. Prove us Your humble vessels. We claim it as done. So be it.

Galatians 5:19-23 Now the works of the flesh are manifest, which are

these; Adultery, fornication, uncleanness, lasciviousness, Idolatry,
witchcraft, hatred, variance, emulations, wrath, strife, seditions,
heresies, Envyings, murders, drunkenness, revellings, and such like: of
the which I tell you before, as I have also told you in time past, that they
which do such things shall not inherit the kingdom of God. But the fruit
of the Spirit is love, joy, peace, longsuffering, gentleness, goodness, faith,
Meekness, temperance: against such there is no law.

1 Corinthians 6:20For ye are bought with a price: therefore glorify God
in your body, and in your spirit, which are God's.

Day 19

Father we come to You in humility. But also with the boldness that Your
word we says we can come before You as Your children. We come with
praise and thanksgiving in our hearts. We ask for Your grace and mercy to
cover us in forgiveness. Please forgive us of all we have thought , said, or
displayed that has displeased You in any way. We ask for forgiveness on
behalf of our ancestors, Father. We also come to You asking forgiveness on
behalf of our fallen and falling heads of Israel. Father, You are the Healer of
the brokenhearted. You declare that You bind up their wounds. Because it is

Your nature to heal, we ask You to heal of all our emotional wounds as well as theirs. By Your love and power, remove any hurt and anger that we are experiencing. Not just us, the women, Father, but the heads, and our children as well. Help all of us to move on tol wholeness of spirit, soul, and body. Father, we ask that as a nation we would trust in You as our Healer. Build our faith to depend on You as THE Healer. Reveal that You are filled with mercy and grace. Convict every one of Your children of Your willingness and ability to heal. Father, You are their Creator just as You are ours. You have made our emotions. These emotions have been wounded; they have been torn apart. Wicked, unrighteous emotions have been cultivated into our lives. We plead for You to release Your power into our lives. Remove the wicked, unrighteous emotions that resulted from our emotional wounds. Heal us so that we all can experience emotional health and wholeness. Father, each one of us has experienced deep emotional wounds. But we ask now that You to deliver us out of

all of these. Heal us and cause us to grow from these wounds. Father, You promise to be near those who are brokenhearted. We call on that promise because we know that You are not a man that You should lie. But many times in our brokenness we do not draw near to You as we should. We run away from You in shame and defeat and unworthiness. Father bring us near. Especially the ones of us who are plagued with shame and guilt. Allow them to feel Your love and forgiveness. Expose them to Your plan for their life even through their mistakes and failures. Show them how You will use their failures and brokenness to gain the glory. We pray that You would grant each of us a deeper experience of Your presence. Surround us with Your love. Cause each one of Your children to know that You love them without reservation. Father, You sent the Messiah to set the captives free. We pray that every sister and brother in bondage would be set free from every past hurt that binds him/her. Father, we ask that You would bind Satan and his demons from tormenting each of us and causing us to believe the lie that we are no longer wanted by You and can not come to You in prayer for forgiveness. We plead that these demons would no longer have the opportunity to harass or oppress us through our emotional wounds. Deliver us from the attacks of the enemy through each and every past emotional wounds. Heal us and cut off every avenue of the enemy in our lives. Protect us and defend us as You said You would Father. Send warring angels to fight on our behalf. Send ministering angels and righteous influences to interfere in the enemy's plans. Let Your plan and Your will be sovereign. We plead that each afflicted sibling would seek You with all his/her heart. Draw them to You. Let the Holy spirit minister to them . Let them be unable to ignore Your voice Father and where ever they turn let them be reminded of Your love and see your face. Let them run to You for the peace they long for. We ask that they would cry out to You for healing. We seek You with all that we are and pray that You would release Your healing into our lives. Father, we ask You to set us free from any unforgiveness in our hearts. Uncover, uproot, and deeply convict us of any unforgiveness that we are harboring. Through Your grace and power, enable us to release the debt, the anger, and the damage into Your hands. Help us to forgive as You do for the sake of Christ. Father, grant us the strength and help us to face the wounds of the past. Help us not neglect or suppress the hurt or the pain. Empower us to face these things, to seek You for healing, and move on by Your grace and power. We pray that our past would no longer hurt, hinder, or destroy our present and future. Father, we pray that You would cultivate the fruit of Spirit in our lives. We plead with You to transform us Father. Root out the wicked, negative, and unrighteous emotions that have been cultivated in our lives. Replace these things with Your fruit. Father, we have been wounded. Yet, we plead to You for Your healing in each of our lives. We ask that You would cause each of us to forget those things that happened in the past and make it possible for us to press on to Your purpose and Your blessings for our future. Create in us a clean heart. Renew in us a right spirit. Break every mental stronghold. Make us over Father. Help us to keep our eyes focused on You. Help us to continue to seek You and experience to the fullest what You have purposed for each of our lives. We ask You to deal with any sinful attitudes or behaviors in our lives that would hinder our relationships. We plead that You would grant us healthy, godly relationships. Remove anger and hatred and replace it with love. Remove depression and despair and replace it with joy. Remove fear and anxiety and replace it with peace. Remove resentment and temper and replace it with longsuffering. Remove bitterness and a critical spirit and replace it with kindness. Remove selfishness and replace it with goodness. Fill the wounded with Your love; show Your concern. Manifest Your power and grace by healing and blessing. And according to Your word Father we call out speaking Your words to these dry bones. O ye dry bones, hear the word of the Lord.Thus saith the Lord God unto these bones; Behold, I will cause breath to enter into you, and ye shall live. And I will lay sinews upon you, and will bring up flesh upon you, and cover you with skin, and put breath in you, and ye shall live; and ye shall know that I am the Lord.Thus saith the Lord God; Come from the four winds, O breath, and breathe upon these slain, that they may live. Son of man, these bones are the whole house of Israel: behold, they say, Our bones are dried, and our hope is lost: we are cut off for our parts. Behold, O my people, I will open your graves, and cause you to come up out of your graves, and bring you into the land of Israel.And ye shall know that I am the Lord, when I have opened your graves, O my people, and brought you up out of your graves,And shall put my spirit in you, and ye shall live, and I shall place you in your own land: then shall ye know that I the Lord have spoken it, and performed it, saith the Lord. You have spoken it and it shall be done. We wait in expectation Father, for You to perform it. We claim it in Your power and Your might. So be it.

Psalms 147:3 He healeth the broken in heart, and bindeth up their wounds.

Psalms 34:18 The LORD [is] nigh unto them that are of a broken heart; and saveth such as be of a contrite spirit.

Numbers 23:19 God is not a man, that he should lie; neither the son of man, that he should repent: hath he said, and shall he not do it? or hath he spoken, and shall he not make it good?

Isaiah 61 The Spirit of the Lord God is upon me; because the Lord hath anointed me to preach good tidings unto the meek; he hath sent me to bind up the brokenhearted, to proclaim liberty to the captives, and the opening of the prison to them that are bound;

Psalm 51:10 Create in me a clean heart, O God; and renew a right spirit within me.

Ezekiel 37:4-6 Again he said unto me, Prophesy upon these bones, and say unto them, O ye dry bones, hear the word of the Lord. THus saith the Lord God unto these bones; Behold, I will cause breath to enter into you, and ye shall live: And I will lay sinews upon you, and will bring up flesh upon you, and cover you with skin, and put breath in you, and ye shall live; and ye shall know that I am the Lord

Ezekiel 37:11-13 Then he said unto me, Son of man, these bones are the whole house of Israel:behold, they say, Or bones are dried, and our hope

is lost: we are cut off for our parts. Therefore prophesy and say unto them, Thus saith the Lord God; Behold, O my people, I will open your graves, and cause you to come up out of your graves, and bring you into the land of Israel. And ye shall know that I am the Lord, when I have opened your graves, O my people, and brought you up out of your graves.

Day 20

Father thank you for waking us up this morning and giving us another day to praise your Holy name. We thank you for your many mercies. We ask for forgiveness for any thought, word, or deed we have displeased you with. Please have mercy on our behalf for the sins of our ancestors and even the sins of our heads. For You Father, are good, and ready to forgive; and plenteous in mercy unto all them that call upon You. Bow down thine ear, O Most High, hear us: for we are poor and needy. Preserve our souls, save Your servants that trusts in You. Be merciful unto us Father for we cry unto You daily. Father we ask that nothing separate us from You today. Teach us Your way, Most High and we will walk in Your truth. Unite our hearts to fear thy name. Teach us how to choose only Your way today so each step will lead us closer to You. Help us walk by the Word and not our feelings. Help us to keep our hearts pure and undivided. Protect us from our own careless thoughts, words, and actions. Protect us from the thoughts and deceptions planted in our minds by the enemy. Keep us from being distracted by our wants, our desires, our thoughts on how things should be. Help us to continuously submit to Your will and to walk in Your way. Help us to speak Your words and think holy thoughts. Your word says You will keep in perfect peace him whose mind is steadfast, because he trusts in You. So we keep our mind stayed on You Father that You may bless us with the peace that passes all understanding. Help us to glorify You in everything that we do. Help us to embrace each task or obstacle that comes our way as an opportunity for growth and service... rather than a personal inconvenience. Let us see the comfort in our discomfort. The blessings in the adversities. Help us to embrace anything that comes our way as an opportunity to see You at work and as an opportunity to point others to You. Help us to rest in Your truth. For great is thy mercy toward us: and thou hast delivered our souls from the lowest hell. We don't know who or what will cross our paths today, but we do know that You are our Rock and our Fortress. You are our Shield and our Strong Tower. We will praise You, O Most High our Power, with all our hearts and we will glorify Your name for evermore. Help us to anchor ourselves to You today. Teach us how to stand strong in You and choose only Your way today. Thank You that You love us and nothing can ever take that away from us! For You are full of compassion, and gracious, long suffering, and plenteous in mercy and truth. Even if we fail or fall short today and somehow disappoint You, Your unconditional and steadfast love continuously pours into our souls.. It never ceases and reminds us that Your mercies are new every morning. Great is thy faithfulness! Give us strength in our weakness. Give us faith in our fear. Give us power in our powerlessness. We are trusting You. When we are tempted to give up, help us to keep going. Grant us a cheerful spirit when things don't go our way. And give us courage to do whatever needs to be done. For You have not given us a spirit of fear, but a spirit of power, of love and sound mind. We ask that You enlarge our territory. That Your mighty hand be with us. That You keep us from evil. That we may not cause pain. We thank You for everything You have provided for us thus far. For everything You have protected us from. For everything You have prepared for us. We stand in expectancy of what's to come knowing that it is for the good of us who love You. We claim every promise You have made and wait on the manifestation of it in the flesh for it has already been done in the spirit. We love You Father . So be it.

Psalm 86 Bow down thine ear, O Lord, hear me: for I am poor and needy.Preserve my soul; for I am holy: O thou my God, save thy servant that trusteth in thee.Be merciful unto me, O Lord: for I cry unto thee daily. Rejoice the soul of thy servant: for unto thee, O Lord, do I lift up my soul.For thou, Lord, art good, and ready to forgive; and plenteous in mercy unto all them that call upon thee. Give ear, O Lord, unto my prayer; and attend to the voice of my supplications. In the day of my trouble I will call upon thee: for thou wilt answer me. Among the gods there is none like unto thee, O Lord; neither are there any works like unto thy works. All nations whom thou hast made shall come and worship before thee, O Lord; and shall glorify thy name. For thou art great, and doest wondrous things: thou art God alone. Teach me thy way, O Lord; I will walk in thy truth: unite my heart to fear thy name.I will praise thee, O Lord my God, with all my heart: and I will glorify thy name for evermore. For great is thy mercy toward me: and thou hast delivered my soul from the lowest hell. O God, the proud are risen against me, and the assemblies of violent men have sought after my soul; and have not set thee before them. But thou, O Lord, art a God full of compassion, and gracious, long suffering, and plenteous in mercy and truth. O turn unto me, and have mercy upon me; give thy strength unto thy servant, and save the son of thine handmaid. Shew me a token for good; that they which hate me may see it, and be ashamed: because thou, Lord, hast holpen me, and comforted me.

Psalm 18:2 The Lord is my rock, and my fortress, and my deliverer; my God, my strength, in whom I will trust; my buckler, and the horn of my

salvation, and my high tower.

2 Timothy 1:7 For God hath not given us the spirit of fear; but of power, and of love, and of a sound mind.

1 Chronicles 4:9-10 And Jabez was more honourable than his brethren: and his mother called his name Jabez, saying, Because I bare him with sorrow. And Jabez called on the God of Israel, saying, Oh that thou wouldest bless me indeed, and enlarge my coast, and that thine hand might be with me, and that thou wouldest keep me from evil, that it may not grieve me! And God granted him that which he requested.

Day 21

Father, thank You for today, a new day, a chance for a new start. Yesterday is gone and with it any regrets, mistakes, or failures we may have experienced. It's a good day to be grateful and to give thanks, and we do, Father. Thank You for today, a new opportunity to love, give, and be all that You want us to be.Today we start the day with you on our minds and in our hearts. We ask for dividend for anything we did to displease You knowingly or unknowingly. We ask for forgiveness on behalf of our ancestors and our heads. We plead for mercy and grace Father. We come before you with open hands and open hearts, depending solely on You to help us through the day and all it will bring our way. As we dress, we put on the armor You provided for us daily: the helmet of salvation, the breastplate of righteousness, the shield of faith, the belt of truth, the sandals of peace, and the sword of the spirit—with prayer on our tongues: praise for You and petitions for those around us and those we meet. Feed us today with Your daily bread. As the Bread of Life, Your food, like manna, will sustain us throughout any trials and hungers. Help us to set our thoughts on things above and to speak only what will help and encourage others. Keep us from dishonoring You with our mouths, and help us guard the affections of our hearts today, Father. Let the work of our hands be marked with Your excellence, as we seek not to make a name for ourselves but to glorify Your Holy name, and to make a difference in Your kingdom. Help us to treat each person we encounter as You would, with respect and love, forgiving others and asking for forgiveness ourselves when needed. As we start this day, help us remember that we belong to You, and our desire is to act accordingly. Keep our feet from stumbling and our mind from wandering into distractions that could steal precious time and energy from the most important things You have designed for us.

We pray You would move the Spirit more boldly in our lives. We know that any sin can grieve and diminish the voice of the Spirit, and we pray against the temptation to sin. Help us crave Your presence more than we crave to please our flesh. Help us grow in the fruit of the Spirit and walk closer with You. We pray for guidance from Your Spirit. Let Your will and promises always be the only meditation of our hearts. Help us be like Nehemiah, to come to You for guidance, strength, provision and protection. As we face tough choices and hard situations, help us remember that we are Your children and Your representative to the world. Help us live today in a way that only brings honor to Your holy name. Help us to remember that every trial that comes our way has already been known to You in advance. We know that You are with us. We are grateful for all You have provided us and allow us to always remember that You are in control. Allow us to learn more every day to be content with life in the moment because You are showing us Your grace and mercy daily. We will persevere through these trials, Father, because You are with us! Thank you for being patient with us as You are growing our patience through our afflictions. We lay before You our tiredness and ask for new energy.We lay before You any frustration and ask for more patience.We lay before You any known or unknown resentments and ask for peace.We lay before You judgement, anger, or any unforgiveness and ask for the ability to be forgiving and understanding. With everything inside of us we believe in You, Your might, and Your power and ability. Let our faith be strong as we move forward in our lives with a total reliance on You. We will not falter or fail for You are with us. We place our total and unconditional trust in You. We believe in Your power of absolute good working on our behalf at all times. We trust in You through any change we may experience. We trust in You through any seeming loss. We trust that whenever anything is eliminated from our lives it is a prelude to better good. We stand in faith by letting go of the old and waiting with open arms and mind for Your goodness. Comfort us with Your peace. Help us to be a blessing. Guide us with Your Wisdom. Prepare us to move forward, unafraid, knowing that You go ahead of us. We thank You for it in advance. So be it.

Ephesians 6:10-18 Finally, my brethren, be strong in the Lord, and in the power of his might.Put on the whole armour of God, that ye may be able to stand against the wiles of the devil. For we wrestle not against flesh and blood, but against principalities, against powers, against the rulers of the darkness of this world, against spiritual wickedness in high places. Wherefore take unto you the whole armour of God, that ye may be able to withstand in the evil day, and having done all, to stand. Stand therefore, having your loins girt about with truth, and having on the breastplate of righteousness;And your feet shod with the preparation of the gospel of peace; Above all, taking the shield of faith, wherewith ye shall be able to quench all the fiery darts of the wicked. And take the helmet of salvation, and the sword of the Spirit, which is the word of God. Praying always with all prayer and supplication in the Spirit, and watching thereunto with all perseverance and supplication for all saints;

Colossians 3:2 Set your affection on things above, not on things on the earth.

Day 22

Almighty Father, thank You for this day. Thank You for waking us up this morning. We know it is a privilege that we are blessed to see another day. We ask for forgiveness for anything we may have done to displease You. We ask for forgiveness on behalf of our ancestors and the heads of Israel. Please have mercy on us Father. We thank You for being the fountain of all wisdom. You know our necessities before we ask. Have compassion on our weakness, and mercifully give us those things which for our unworthiness we dare not, and for our blindness we cannot ask. Grant us Your will and have mercy as You receive the prayers of your people who call upon You. Grant that we may know and understand what things we ought to do, and also allow us to have grace and power faithfully to accomplish Your works. You have taught us to keep all your commandments, laws, and statutes by loving you and our neighbor as we love ourselves. Grant us the grace of your Holy Spirit, that we may be devoted to you with our whole heart, and united to one another with pure love. We realize that as your children our bodies are the temple of the Holy Spirit. We acknowledge Your presence and Your power. We pray that on a daily basis our faith in You grows stronger. We believe that You, heavenly Father, are leading and guiding us by the Holy Spirit through truth, restoring our hearts and minds and leading us into all knowledge, wisdom, and understanding. As we yield to the Holy Spirit, we believe that our steps are ordered of You, Father. We commit, trust, and submit wholly to Your guidance, expecting You to cause our thoughts to become agreeable to Your will, so our plans will be established and succeed. We trust in You, Father with all our hearts and lean not to our own understanding. As we acknowledge You. You direct us in paths of righteousness. We confess that as we become more truth filled and like minded, we can more easily recognize the inward witness of the Holy Spirit. Keep our ears open to hear the voice of the Shepherd, and a stranger's voice we will not follow. We are aware that our spirit is the candle of The Most High. Let our light always burn bright before men that You may get all the glory. Keep us meditating in Your WORD day and night, not letting it depart from our mouths. Allow us to be quick to act on The WORD, as well as the prompting of our spirits. We are not hearers only, but also doers of Your word. Therefore, we shall be blessed in all our deeds. May Your truth be the lamp that lights our way and brings us clarity. May Your love be a compass that gives us direction. May Your fruit be the measure that guides our decisions. May Your peace be the breeze that cools our spirits and keeps us refreshed. May our words be in our minds, and our hearts, and our mouths continuously. We ask all these things in Your power and Your might. We wait in expectancy for them all to be perfected in the flesh as they have already come to pass in the spirit. We thank You for your provision, protection , and providence. We thank You for everything You have done, are doing, and what is yet to come. We claim every promise You have made us and we thank You in advance. For it is already done. So be it.

1 Corinthians 6:15-20 Know ye not that your bodies are the members of Christ? shall I then take the members of Christ, and make them the members of an harlot? God forbid. What? know ye not that he which is joined to an harlot is one body? for two, saith he, shall be one flesh.But

he that is joined unto the Lord is one spirit.Flee fornication. Every sin that a man doeth is without the body; but he that committeth fornication sinneth against his own body. What? know ye not that your body is the temple of the Holy Ghost which is in you, which ye have of God, and ye are not your own? For ye are bought with a price: therefore glorify God in your body, and in your spirit, which are God's.

Day 23

Heavenly Father we come to You today with Thanksgiving in our hearts and praise on our lips. You are so awesome Father. You are more than worthy to be praised. First we come to You in humility pleading Your forgiveness for any trespass we have thought, spoken, or performed against You. We ask for forgiveness on behalf of our ancestors and we plead on behalf of our heads, the leaders of Israel. We plead Your grace and mercy over their lives and ours. Father we thank You for Your graciousness and the loving kindness You provide that we could never deserve. We thank You for Your providence. Thank You for considering us when we don't even consider You. Thank You for considering us when we don't even consider ourselves. Thank You for taking the time to set Your plans toward us in motion before we were even birth. Thank You that You are taking the time to cleanse and perfect us. We are so filthy Father even in our righteousness. We long to be perfect in Your sight. We could never deserve all You have planned for us. We thank You for loving us, chastising us, molding us. Thank You for choosing us Father. You didn't have to. Out of the billions of people you could have chosen, You chose us. Out of all the nations You chose ours. After all of our backsliding You stayed faithful, and patiently waiting for us to return to You. Thank You for staying true to Your word even though we didn't. For protecting us even from ourselves. From the times when we were in sin and headed towards destruction. Thank You for keeping us from destroying ourselves, from dying in our wickedness. We thank You Father for protecting us from attacks and pitfalls we could not see. Thank You for letting us fall and picking us up. Thank You for providing for us. For providing every one of our needs. Even when we thought we were providing for ourselves outside of You. We can't thank You enough. We praise You for Your ways that are not our ways because if they were we wouldn't have You. We praise You and thank You for Your thoughts so much higher and perfectly pure in comparison to our thoughts. Thank You for Your spirit that comforts us now , and leads us into all knowledge, truth, wisdom, and holy understanding. Thank You for the strength You provide us in our weakness. Thank You for the things You have allowed that we have yet to understand. Keep us from leaning to our own understanding. We long to stay focused on You. Our eyes, ears, minds stayed in You. Our feet on Your path. Our hands about Your work. Our mouths filled with Your words. Help us to honor You, Father. To give You the glory in every action of these vessels. Allow us to be used for Your purpose. We submit to Your will Father. Keep us in Your way. We relinquish our will and our wants and desires for Yours Father. Not our will but Yours be done. In all things, and through everything, each trial, each storm, in expectancy of the sunshine. We hope to see Your kingdom. We long to please You and hear well done. We claim every promise that You have made. We trust You and know that You have never and will never let us down. We know that your word will not return to you void. All that you set forth shall be accomplished. Thank You for all You have done, are doing, and will do. So be it.

Isaiah 55:8-13 For my thoughts are not your thoughts, neither are your ways my ways, saith the Lord. For as the heavens are higher than the

earth, so are my ways higher than your ways, and my thoughts than your thoughts. For as the rain cometh down, and the snow from heaven, and returneth not thither, but watereth the earth, and maketh it bring forth and bud, that it may give seed to the sower, and bread to the eater: So shall my word be that goeth forth out of my mouth: it shall not return unto me void, but it shall accomplish that which I please, and it shall prosper in the thing whereto I sent it.

Day 24

Father we come before you in humility bowing before You and Your glorious throne of grace. We ask for forgiveness for anything we have done against you knowingly or unknowingly. We all for forgiveness of our ancestors and our heads. Father we please that You continue to extend Your grace and mercy to us. Cleanse us Father of all unrighteousness. Protect us in this wicked world. Many hearts are bound by ego and fear. Please strengthen our faith in Your higher purpose and open our minds to the truth that everything is unfolding according to Your divine plan. Let compassion and love for my brothers and sisters flow from us and may we all be uplifted by your glory. We lift up our eyes to the hills from whence comes our help. Our help comes from You O Most High, who made heaven and earth. Your word says You will not allow our feet to be moved; You who keeps us will not slumber.

Behold, You who keeps Israel shall neither slumber nor sleep. The MOST HIGH is our keeper; The MOST HIGH is our shade at our right hand. The sun shall not strike us by day, Nor the moon by night. You shall preserve us from all evil; You shall preserve our souls. The Most High shall preserve our going out and our coming in From this time forth, and even forevermore. Father, it is in our weaknesses that Your power is made most visible in our lives. We call out for deliverance and yet endure the discomfort and affliction as a true soldier of the faith, all the while being joyful in hope, patient in affliction and faithful in prayer. Father, it is under Your wings that we are protected against the fierce wind currents of doubt, fear, and impatience. Such troubling emotions weigh us down and can pull us right into the path of a pelting storm. But it is through eyes of faith and a heart of trust that we can mount up with You and soar like eagles above the assaulting storm. You promise never to leave us nor forsake us which gives us courage to wait and trust You to fully answer our prayers. Father, Help us to work through these jolts of the unexpected and unwelcome interruptions that bring sadness, disappointment or a change of our seemingly perfect plans. It's how You work Your purpose in our lives as we overcome and work through major obstacles that affect us. We seek to remain steadfast, moving forward in our walk as we experience the inevitable heartaches of life. At times we bring about our own grief and troubles because of our unrighteous actions. We thank You for Your forgiveness in these matters. You give us fresh resolve to trust and obey You. Thank You that You are the God of the impossible. You can do anything. We trust in Your ability and not our own. Teach us to see difficulties in our lives from Your perspective. Help us to focus on You and Your power. Help us to be like Joshua and Caleb who believed in a good report and focused on You even in hard circumstances (Numbers 14:7-9). Today we bring before You every difficulty in our lives. Help us not to fear but to trust You in each situation. We declare our faith in Your ability to fulfill Your promises to us. You will fight for us and win the battles in our lives. You are mighty, powerful, righteous and true. We have nothing to fear with You on my side. We will be strong and courageous even in hard times. We will not be terrified or discouraged, for the Most High will be with us wherever we go. You will never leave or forsake us. We do not need to figure everything out. You already know the best plan for our lives. We will not try any man-made method to do only what You can do. Show us Your supernatural power, Your mighty hand. Teach us how to walk by faith and pray breakthrough prayers. We choose to have faith in Your ability to break through every obstacle in our lives. Just like Joshua, You will give is the land and every place where our feet step. Through thee will we push down our enemies: through thy name will we tread them under that rise up against us. For I will not trust in my bow, neither shall my sword save me.But thou hast saved us from our enemies, and hast put them to shame that hated us. In God we boast all the day long, and praise thy name for ever. Lord, you have assigned me my portion and my cup; you have made my lot secure. The boundary lines have fallen for me in pleasant places; surely I have a delightful inheritance. I will praise the Lord, who counsels me; even at night my heart instructs me. I have set the Lord always before me. Because he is at my right hand, I will not be shaken. Therefore my heart is glad and my tongue rejoices; my body also will rest secure, because you will not abandon me to the grave, nor will you let your Holy One see decay. You have made known to me the path of life; you will fill me with joy in your presence, with eternal pleasures at your right hand. We thank You for everything You are doing. We thank You for everything You have done. We thank You for Your plans pertaining to us and Your promises. We appreciate Your provision and Your protection. We submit to Your Providence. We claim everything promised to us and we wait on these things expectantly. It is already done. So be it.

Psalm121 I will lift up mine eyes unto the hills, from whence cometh my help.My help cometh from the Lord, which made heaven and earth.He will not suffer thy foot to be moved: he that keepeth thee will not slumber.Behold, he that keepeth Israel shall neither slumber nor sleep.The Lord is thy keeper: the Lord is thy shade upon thy right hand.The sun shall not smite thee by day, nor the moon by night.The Lord shall preserve thee from all evil: he shall preserve thy soul. The Lord shall preserve thy going out and thy coming in from this time forth, and even for evermore.

Joshua 1:9 Have not I commanded thee? Be strong and of a good courage; be not afraid, neither be thou dismayed: for the LORD thy God is with thee whithersoever thou goest.

Joshua 1:5 There shall not any man be able to stand before thee all the days of thy life: as I was with Moses, so I will be with thee: I will not fail thee, nor forsake thee.

Joshua 1:3 Every place that the sole of your foot shall tread upon, that have I given unto you, as I said unto Moses.

Psalm 44:5-8Through thee will we push down our enemies: through thy name will we tread them under that rise up against us. For I will not trust in my bow, neither shall my sword save me.But thou hast saved us from our enemies, and hast put them to shame that hated us. In God we boast all the day long, and praise thy name for ever.

Psalms 16:5-11Lord, you have assigned me my portion and my cup; you have made my lot secure. The boundary lines have fallen for me in pleasant places; surely I have a delightful inheritance. I will praise the Lord, who counsels me; even at night my heart instructs me. I have set the Lord always before me. Because he is at my right hand, I will not be shaken. Therefore my heart is glad and my tongue rejoices; my body also will rest secure, because you will not abandon me to the grave, nor will you let your Holy One see decay. You have made known to me the path of life; you will fill me with joy in your presence, with eternal pleasures at your right hand

Day 25

Father we come to You today in complete reverence. We bow before You knowing we are not worthy to be in Your presence. We humbly ask for Your grace and mercy. Please forgive us for any trespass we may have done against you. Forgive us for any thoughts that were grievous. Any ought we have hidden in our hearts. Any actions we have made against Your will. Forgive us for acting of our own accord. Forgive us for making our own plans, for repeatedly giving you our problems and then taking them back. Forgive us for our disobedience. For pledging our submission, then going astray. Forgive us for leaning unto our own understanding. Forgive us for thinking we know better than You, for acting without Your permission, for not heading your warnings , and for not keeping our vows to You. Forgive us for not being diligent to the responsibilities You have given us. Forgive us for not staying to Your path of righteousness Father. And while we point fingers at others not forgiving them we still ask for forgiveness. Allow us to let go of any grudges or any judgements we have issued against our brothers and sisters. We ask that You forgive them and give us a measure of your grace and mercy towards them as well. Forgive us for not operating at all times in love and for not having unshakable faith. Forgive us for falling short of our roles as sisters, mother's, and wives. Forgive us for not covering others. Forgive us for only thinking of ourselves and not being the servants You have created us to be. Help us to be selfless Father. Forgive our fallen heads for abandoning their posts. Forgive them for falling under the weight of their responsibilities and not leaning on you. Forgive them for not cleaving to their bodies and to You. Forgive them for falling victim to pride and fear. Forgive them for being victim to anger and blame. Forgive them for wallowing in their weakness, for being led astray by deceit instead of believing in Your truth. Forgive them for walking the path of darkness instead of clinging to your light. Help them to find their way back to you. Help us all to accept Your forgiveness and to correct our wrongs. We plead for You to shine Your magnificent light so we can find and stay on the path of righteousness. Send your Holy spirit to lead, guide, and direct us. We long to please you Father. Help us to crucify our flesh and completely submit ourselves to You. Your word says in Romans 8:28-33 And we know that all things work together for good to them that love God, to them who are the called according to his purpose. For whom he did foreknow, he also did predestinate to be conformed to the image of his Son, that he might be the firstborn among many brethren.Moreover whom he did predestinate, them he also called: and whom he called, them he also justified: and whom he justified, them he also glorified.What shall we then say to these things? If God be for us, who can be against us? He that spared not his own Son, but delivered him up for us all, how shall he not with him also freely give us all things? It says that You knew us before our birth and that You chose and ordained us to be just like Your son who was holy and obedient even unto death. That He was our righteous example and because You choose us for this task You also called us out of the wicked world and freed us from our bondage. Then being freed You also change us and impart us with worth. It also says that if You love us enough to give us the example of Your son, what things would You withhold from us. It asks the question if You the Father and creator of all be for those of us who You have chosen than who or what could be against us. Which is why all things Must work together for the good of us who were called because Your purpose is good and therefore everything must contribute to that same goodness. Help us to hold on to this Father. In the face of this adversity and these trials it is difficult to stay mindful of the goodness that is to come. It is hard to stay joyful and to find peace. Help us to rest in Your embrace and find comfort in Your assurance Father. You know the ending of our race Father. You are more than sure You are certain. Allow us to rest in Your knowledge and not our own. Cover us with Your confidence. Let the peace that passes all understanding encompass us and keep our hearts and minds secure. Your word says You are our provider, our protection, our defense. So help us to rest in Your provision because You know what we need. Help us rest is Your protection because You can see what we can't. Help us rest Father. Help us allow You to do Your job. We thank you for everything You have done, are doing, and will do all for Your glory. We praise You for all You are and all You have done already. We claim our position in Your family and we commit to obedience. Let Your will be done. So be it.

Romans 8:28-33 And we know that all things work together for good to them that love God, to them who are the called according to his purpose. For whom he did foreknow, he also did predestinate to be conformed to the image of his Son, that he might be the firstborn among many brethren.Moreover whom he did predestinate, them he also called: and whom he called, them he also justified: and whom he justified, them he

also glorified.What shall we then say to these things? If God be for us, who can be against us?He that spared not his own Son, but delivered him up for us all, how shall he not with him also freely give us all things? Who shall lay any thing to the charge of God's elect? It is God that justifieth.

Philippians 4:7 And the peace of God, which passeth all understanding, shall keep your hearts and minds through Christ Jesus.

Day 26

Heavenly Father, the wonder of whose presence fills us with awe. Closer to us than our own hearts, yet farther from us than the most distant star. Most High, lover of us all, most Holy one. You love us like a good parent, and are present in every aspect of our existence. Let Your will be our will;You will that we be sisters and brothers. Let us recognize that every thought and thing belongs to You. Allow us to create what You want for us here on earth. May Your nature become known and respected by all through us and our actions. May we honor and praise You to Your satisfaction . Fill us with Your creativity, so that we may be empowered to bear the fruit of Your vision. Soften the ground of our being, and hallow in us a space for the planting of Your presence. May we be used by You to establish Your new order of justice, peace and love. Let each of our actions bear fruit in accordance with Your desire. May Your joy, peace, wholeness and justice be the reality for everyone as we live Your way. Let Your kindness, justice and love shine in our lives. May we move from separation toward union, to live in abundance of grace and mercy with love in our hearts. Empower us with creativity, and clothe us with royal dignity. May we find we have all we need to meet each day without unnecessary anxiety .Give us what we need, day by day,to keep body and soul together, because clever as you have made us, we still owe our existence to You.Give us all that we really need to live every day for You. We recognize that to be reconciled with You, we must live peaceably and justly with other human beings, putting hate and bitterness behind us. Grant that we may renew each other with love, and understanding. Empty us of frustrated hopes and despair, as we restore others to a renewal of vision. Let us this day sow grace and peace, and show mercy to all, and gentle loving-kindness.And forgive us our failures as we forgive others for their failures. In the hurts we absorb from one another, forgive us.Lighten our load of secret debts as we relieve others of their need to repay.Keep us from hoarding false wealth, and from the inner shame of help not given in time. Let us not be self-serving, but a constant source of giving. Keep us from doing those things which are not of You, and cause us always to be centered on Your love. We are torn between our faith in Your goodness and our awareness of the evil in this world, so deliver us from the temptation to despair.In times of temptation and test, spare us.From the grip of all that is evil, free us.Protect us from pride and from despair and from the fear and hate which can swallow us up. Let us not be captive to uncertainty, nor cling to fruitless pursuits.Do not let us lose ourselves in distraction, but by the way of Your breath, lead us into mindfulness. Strengthen us that we will reach out to the best, always with the faith to rise above the ugly realities of our existence. And we celebrate the gifts you have given us: the rich kingdom of a righteous life full of possibilities, the power to do good and the triumphs of good, and the moments when we have seen Your glory .For You are the ground of the fruitful vision, the birthing-power, and the fulfilment of all goodness. For you are the true reality in this our present, and in all our future.Yours alone is the universe and all its majesty and beauty.In You are truth, meaning, glory and power. For You reign in the glory of the power that is love, now and forever. We claim every promise of our heritage. We claim the blessings of our forefather Abraham, passed down from generation to generation, as we stand a set apart nation, and a Royal priesthood. We wait in expectancy for Your power to perform the works that will bring us to fulfill the expected destiny You have prepared for us. We thank You for it all in advance. For it is Your word and It is done. So be it.

1 Peter 2:9 But ye are a chosen generation, a royal priesthood, an holy nation, a peculiar people; that ye should shew forth the praises of him who hath called you out of darkness into his marvellous light

Day 27

Heavenly Father thank You for another day. We come before Your throne of grace boldly that we may receive grace and mercy in our time of need. Forgive us of all unrighteousness. We fall on our faces before You asking forgiveness for every thought, word, and deed that was not brought into submission of You. Forgive us for our weaknesses and forgive our heads and our ancestors for going astray. We thank You for the opportunity to enter Your presence. We thank You for even considering and hearing our prayers. We are grateful that we have been chosen by You for Your wonderful work. Help us to keep focus on our goals and not be sidetracked. We thank You for keeping us safe throughout our days and watching over us as we sleep. Father we thank You for the work you are doing in us. We thank You for the trying, the purifying, the cleansing of all unrighteousness. We know You are our refuge and our fortress and helper. We have no fear of any weapon or man that would come against us, for with You on our side whom shall we fear. Father we ask that You send warring angels to fight on our behalf. To fight on behalf of the brothers and sisters that have gone astray and are under attack. Your word says that You are our provider and protector and that You war against the enemy on our behalf, so we ask because we know You keep Your promises. We ask that You defend them from the clutches of the enemy. That You lovingly bring them back to You and chastise them for their shortcomings. We ask that You not do away with them and leave them to the devices of the adversary although they have turned against Your word in disobedience. We ask this because we know you love them. They are Your chosen sons and daughters Father and we know that whom You love You chastise. This is the characteristic of a loving Father and You are beyond loving and patient with us. They need Your correction Father. I know deep down they long to serve You because You have planted the desire to produce Your fruit in them since before their beginning. We ask that you call forth the seeds which were first planted to rise up against all the enemy has planted in them to cause them to rebel and turn against what is righteous and true and all that rightfully belongs to them as Your children. We thank You that You are healing that which is broken and straightening the paths that have been made crooked. We thank You that You are the way maker and the Potter. We know that You are in control of all things and that this trial is a part of Your plan. We know that Your word says that all things are for the good of those who love You and we love You Father. We obey Your words. We walk after Your path. This is the reason we come before You with our requests Father. Your word says that we should be long suffering in love and intercede on behalf of a fallen brother. So we cannot leave them behind. We stand in assurance of You Father and have faith that You are performing the impossible on our behalf for Your own glory. We rebuke every attempt, every plot, every interference of the enemy. We bind every demon, every stronghold , every deception that he may use against us. We thank You that Your word assures us that You have chosen us and we cannot be plucked from Your hand. We rest in the assurance that You hold in Your hand the good and the evil and that all bow before You. We know You have an expected end and that which You expect WILL be done. We let go of all fear and anxiety regarding the mending of our spirits, our hearts, our unions and our nation. We stand in prayer, with all faith and confidence in Your ability to perform it. We know You have chosen us to endure and we submit to Your will. We will continue to endure Father. Pour out Your spirit on us and bless us with immeasurable strength and favor. We thank You that our every need and desire is met. We have no lack, for You, our Father, do not operate in lack and brokenness. We thank You for the Holy spirit which leads, guides, directs us, and is with us always blessing us with wisdom and knowledge. Allow us to stay focused on You and the perfection of our spirit. While we intercede for them we ask that you release your fire upon us all. Allow us to be on fire for You because Your word says that we must either be in or out, hot or cold, and if we are lukewarm or double minded we shall receive nothing from You and we will be spit out. So we ask that You stoke our fire and rekindle a raging blaze in Your children that have or are going out. Quicken our spirits Father. Let the calling that You have on them be louder than they can ignore. Trouble their spirits and allow for them to have no peace or comfort in their sin. Let them thirst for you like a dear thirsts for water. Let their hunger for truth and righteousness be unquenchable. Let them be irritated by what once brought them escape from their pain. Make them face their fears Father and show them that You are sovereign over all. Heal their brokenness and expose their flaws and iniquities Father. Tear away the tainted scabs that cover their wounds and allow real healing to take place in them. Let them hide no more. Still their feet from running from their calling and their given positions. Rise up your warriors Father, Your nation of sons who are men after Your own heart, Your nation of virtuous women who are prayer warriors and the sisters, wives, and mothers You created them to be. Let Your might be shown in them and magnified in all the earth. Place us on solid ground that we may worship You with one voice on one accord for all the nations to witness and tremble at the sight. We claim this IS happening. The mountains of rebellion, and fear, deceit, and adversity are crumbling at this very moment for No Thing, No one, No evil shall befall us neither shall any plague come nigh our dwelling and NONE can resist the command of You or us who move in Your power and authority. We call these things which have not yet manifested in the flesh to become as solid in this world as they are already manifested in the spirit world and Your word says what is loosed in this earth is loosed in Heaven. Let Your nation reign Father. Let Your will be sovereign. Let Your kingdom come. Let Your will be done on earth as it already is in heaven. So be it.

Deuteronomy 33:27 The eternal God is your refuge, and underneath are the everlasting arms; He will thrust out the enemy from before you, and will say, 'Destroy!

Isaiah 45:2 I will go before you and make the crooked paths straight; I will break in pieces the gates of bronze and cut the bars of iron.

For thou hast possessed my reins: thou hast covered me in my mother's womb. I will praise thee; for I am fearfully and wonderfully made: marvellous are thy works; and that my soul knoweth right well. My substance was not hid from thee, when I was made in secret, and curiously wrought in the lowest parts of the earth. Thine eyes did see my substance, yet being unperfect; and in thy book all my members were written, which in continuance were fashioned, when as yet there was none of them."

Psalms 139:13-16 Surely your turning of things upside down shall be esteemed as the potter's clay: for shall the work say of him that made it, He made me not? or shall the thing framed say of him that framed it, He had no understanding?

Isaiah 29:16 But now, O LORD, thou art our father; we are the clay, and thou our potter; and we all are the work of thy hand."

Isaiah 64:8 O house of Israel, cannot I do with you as this potter? saith the LORD. Behold, as the clay is in the potter's hand, so are ye in mine

hand, O house of Israel."

Jeremiah 18:6 O house of Israel, cannot I do with you as this potter saith the Lord. Behold, as the clay is in the potter's hand, so are ye in mine hand, O house of Israel.

John 10:27-30 My sheep hear my voice, and I know them, and they follow me: And I give unto them eternal life; and they shall never perish, neither shall any man pluck them out of my hand. My Father, which gave them me, is greater than all; and no man is able to pluck them out of my Father's hand. I and my Father are one.

Revelations 3:15-19 I know thy works, that thou art neither cold nor hot: I would thou wert cold or hot. So then because thou art lukewarm, and neither cold nor hot, I will spue thee out of my mouth.Because thou sayest, I am rich, and increased with goods, and have need of nothing; and knowest not that thou art wretched, and miserable, and poor, and blind, and naked: I counsel thee to buy of me gold tried in the fire, that thou mayest be rich; and white raiment, that thou mayest be clothed, and that the shame of thy nakedness do not appear; and anoint thine eyes with eyesalve, that thou mayest see.As many as I love, I rebuke and chasten: be zealous therefore, and repent.

Psalm 91:10 There shall no evil befall thee, neither shall any plague come nigh thy dwelling.

Matthew 18:18 Verily I say unto you, Whatsoever ye shall bind on earth shall be bound in heaven: and whatsoever ye shall loose on earth shall be loosed in heaven.

Day 28

Abba we come before you in prayer and supplication, kneeling before you in humility and reverence before Your magnificence. We come to You in agreement on behalf of Israel. We come bringing our desires before You with all faith and assurance that You hear our prayers. Father Your word says that the effectual fervent prayers of the righteous availeth much and we are in need of much result and much favor. We know that the enemy is attacking Israel. Attempting to decapitate the head from the body to render us incapable of performing the work You have set before us. Your word also says that when we operate in obedience there is nothing that will be withheld from us, especially if we pray according to Your will. So Father we ask that You show yourself mighty on behalf of your children. Your sons and daughters have fallen and are falling daily to weakness of the spirit. The enemy is preying on them through lusts of the flesh and many spiritual traps and temptations. He has placed before them many pitfalls and they have sunken into unrighteousness in flesh, spirit, and in thought. We desire correction Oh Most High. Your word says those who you love you chasten. We know You love them and have chosen them above all to perform Your will. You have set before each of Your children up for a great responsibility and many have yet to step into the positions You have assigned them. They are far from Your path Father. Correct them. We pray the Holy Spirit falls upon each of us and quicken their spirits. That each one of us be touched in the deepest part of ourselves where the seeds of darkness stay rooted and hidden from their sight. We ask that these seeds be uprooted and destroyed. We take full authority through our obedience over the principalities, powers, rules of darkness, and wickedness in high places that seek to hinder the completion of Your will and purpose for their lives and for the completion of the body of Israel. We rebuke every spirit of pride, low self esteem, disobedience, deception, spiritual blindness, self righteousness , vanity, lust, procrastination, irresponsibility, laziness, anger, malice, condemnation, leviathan, complacency, foolishness, witchcraft, and any other unrighteous unclean entity that seeks to bind us away from our chosen and ordained destiny in Your will. In place of these we call forth humility, integrity, honor, submission, obedience, love, faith, sound mind, wisdom, peace, long suffering, strength of spirit, servitude, and most of all righteousness. We are Your chosen seed, the apple of Your eye Father we plead for Your defense.

We ask that You send Your mighty warring angels to intercede on our behalf; To fight this battle that we are not strong enough to fight on our own. Your word says in our weakness Your strength is glorified. Be thou glorified in this victory Abba . Show Yourself mighty among those that doubt and have lost faith in Your power. Let the salvation and correction of Your children be a testimony to Your everlasting goodness and mercy and loving kindness. Let the enemy tremble in Your presence. We bind each prodigal brother and sister that they find no peace or comfort in their vices, that no outside substance will be able to quiet the voice of the Holy spirit or remove the conviction of their spirit until they submit to You Father. That they have no peaceful sleep, no moment of rest until the thirst for You moves them to obedience. We ask that Your word stay before them all day and night, that they will not be able to turn to the left or right without seeing Your direction. That nowhere they turn will they be able to escape from Your face. Trouble them into submission Father. Let them be fearful before You Father. This is our desire that Your desire be manifested for all to behold. Let this work be done hastily Father. We know You are moving because Your word cannot return void. You stand by word word to hastily perform it and You are not a man that You should ever lie. We have full confidence and faith that You are performing these things as we speak them on one accord. We thank you in advance that it is done. So be it.

James 5:16 Confess your faults one to another, and pray one for another, that ye may be healed. The effectual fervent prayer of a righteous man availeth much.

2 Corinthians 12:9 And he said unto me, My grace is sufficient for thee: for my strength is made perfect in weakness. Most gladly therefore will I rather glory in my infirmities, that the power of Christ may rest upon me.

Jeremiah 1:12 Then said the LORD unto me, Thou hast well seen: for I will hasten my word to perform it.

Matthew 18:19 Again I say unto you, That if two of you shall agree on earth as touching anything that they shall ask, it shall be done for them of my Father which is in heaven.

Day 29

Father we come before you in humility and thanksgiving. Giving You all honor and praise for You alone are worthy. We praise Your holy name for we know that You are the one true Power the Most High God above all, in all, and through all on this earth. We glorify Your holy name Father You are the Great I AM, God of Israel. We thank you for choosing us, for keeping us, for never forsaking us Father. We thank you for providing for us, for proving us, and protecting us. We come before you asking first for forgiveness for any unrighteousness we have committed in Your eyesight. Please forgive us. Have mercy and grace upon us Father. We ask forgiveness on behalf of Israel and our ancestors as well Father. This is our confession, hear our pleas and grant us absolution. Heal our nation Father. We come to You because You are our source. You are our Father. And Your word says that the wicked give to their children how much more would You give to us that we ask for. So we come as Your children. Humbly, in meekness, and temperance. Not asking for earthly riches but riches of spirit. We ask that you will restore our nation Father. We ask that you bring back the order which You originally intended. Your word says that in You all of our needs are met. We need You Father. Your word says that we should not worry about our provision because You provide for us. It also says that You will make a way to escape out of temptation for us. We ask that you forge in us a spirit of obedience even unto death. That we be willing to sacrifice ourselves for Your will Father. We come to You asking for healing Father. For in your word it says that no weapon formed against us shall prosper and that by his stripes we are healed. Your word says that sin is death and You are life. We call for life to the places where the enemy has planted death, Father. We take up the armor You have provided for us as a portion of Your protection for us from the adversary. We put on the breastplate of righteousness and command that every demonic influence that attempts to persuade and influence us to walk in unrighteousness be cast back to the pit of hell. Let there be a continuous thirst for righteousness in us. Let us always thirst to serve You and please you as a deer thirsts for water. Let that thirst be quenched no where else but in You Father. We put on the helmet of salvation. We command that every generational curse, every plot of witchcraft, every addiction, every enemy of salvation be cast down at this very moment. And we take up the shield of faith and we use it to quench every fiery dart the enemy may attempt to throw and use against us. Lastly we take up the sword of the spirit. We speak Your word Father for your word is life and Your word does not fail. We call those things which be not as though they were. We stand here in faith claiming the substance of things hoped for and those things that have not yet manifested in the flesh but are already alive in the spirit, proclaiming the victory in this battle against the children of the Most High. We believe with all assurance and expectancy that our prayers are being answered at this very moment. We rebuke the attacks of the enemy and stand in agreement against the powers of darkness. In You there is no lack Father. We call an end to the season of lack Father. We call this the season of completion , the season of healing, the season of newness, the season of truth. That all these things will abide. That light will prevail, that darkness will cower before Your power Father. We call the things which be not as though they were because we walk by faith and not by sight. We confess that we are more than conquerors. That no weapon formed against us has prospered. That healing and restoration is ours.Remove the mountain adversity. Rebuke the enemy that seeks to rise against Your children and make a mockery of Your name in the earth. These are Your desires for us Your children. We long to live Your desires, Father. We long to be the righteousness You see, and the mirror image for the world to behold. We cannot do this without You. Without You we are empty vessels. Fill us with the love that conquers all. Your word says love covers a multitude of sins. And we stand here asking for You to cover us all with Your love. For without You we are not able to stand. Without You we cannot succeed. We know we are weak but in You we are strong. We plead You stretch forth Your mighty hand. Father we plead for You to fix what is broken, to right what is wrong , to restore what has been stolen. Rise up Your Holy nation Father. Set us in line and on one accord again. Bring home the family members that are still sleeping or have awakened and wandered off the path. Chastens us, prove us, and refine us with fire Father. Justify us that in the end we may be magnified and You will be glorified. We thank You that in serving all of our needs are met. We thank You that in giving we receive. We thank You that in obeying we are blessed beyond measure. We love You Father and we ask not that we receive riches or recognition but that we can complete Your work. We ask that Your perfect will be done in us. We know that we ask according to Your will and it is already so. We stand in assurance of the completion of all we have asked and more. We thank You and praise You for You are wonderful and awesome and we in no way could ever deserve all You have done and are doing in us and through us. With a million tongues we could not thank You enough. Have Your way Father. So be it.

Matthew 7:11 If ye then, being evil, know how to give good gifts unto your children, how much more shall your Father which is in heaven give good things to them that ask him?

Philippians 4:19 But my God shall supply all your need according to his riches in glory by Christ Jesus.

1 Corinthians 10:13 There hath no temptation taken you but such as is common to man: but God is faithful, who will not suffer you to be tempted above that ye are able; but will with the temptation also make a way to escape, that ye may be able to bear it.

Romans 4:17 (As it is written, I have made thee a father of many nations,) before him whom he believed, even God, who quickeneth the dead, and calleth those things which be not as though they were.

2 Corinthians 5:7 (For we walk by faith, not by sight:)

Day 30

Father as we embark on this the last day of our collective prayer we come before You with thanks and praise on our lips . Father we thank You for all that you have given us and plead Your grace and mercy on us for any transgressions we have waged against You. Forgive us for our thoughts, words, and actions that defied Your will. Fortify us with the ability to submit to You completely Father. We ask for forgiveness on behalf of our heads, Father. We also ask for forgiveness on behalf of our ancestors who betrayed their covenant with You. We thank you for all You have done for us. We thank You for giving us another day to get right in Your eyesight. We thank You for the Mountains of discord that You have removed from amongst us. We thank You for moving the mountains that were inside of us Father ; the mountains of pride and separation. We have been joined together in sisterhood and the Holy spirit flows freely among us in wisdom, knowledge, and truth. And we thank you deeply for the unity we feel, the sisterly bond and togetherness that has encompassed us. We thank You for taking the blinders off of our eyes and allowing us to see ourselves through Your eyes Father. Thank You for allowing us to see our flaws. Thank You for giving us Your divine direction that shows us the seeds of disobedience and deceptions that were present in us and purging us of them. Thank You for leading us on the pathway of obedience and righteousness. We thank You and praise You that You take Your time to direct us. For we know Your time is precious and Your timing is perfect. Thank you that You are taking the time to fortify us in your ways Father. We are humbled and so appreciative of Your attention to our needs, to the answering of our prayers. Thank you for the strength to stand when we feel like quitting. Thank you for the strength to endure when the fire seems to get too hot. Conquer every seed of fear that would rise up in us against Your authority. Father we thank You and praise You for using us to bring You joy. In the midst of all the plagues, pressures, and problems we face while in our fleshly bodies, please continue growing us and grooming us into pleasing servants who are always walking in faith of You and obedience to You. Let the Holy Spirit lead us to rest in Your wondrous promises revealed to us through Your Word. Remind us to stand on Your promises for in them lies our provision, protection, providence, and ultimately our victory. We need You Father. We admit that we are weak. Without the strength that You promise us in our weakness we cannot continue, we cannot endure. We do not deserve your grace Father for we have always been a disobedient and stiffnecked nation. We cannot even begin to express our gratitude for the patience, grace, and mercy You have provided us undeservingly again and again. Father we now willingly submit to You and long for the day when we hear you say "Well done good and faithful servant, enter into the kingdom of Your Father." Help us as we continue to grow our faith towards the day that it exceeds much more than a mustard seed but is the very sight we see all things by. We praise you Father for your infinite wisdom. We know nothing, we are nothing in comparison to You, and we are so grateful to be chosen, be used, to serve the Most High God of Israel, the one and only Power who knows all things, and has created all things. There is nothing about us that we can hide. There is nothing about us that you didn't know before You chose us. And we stand before You bare. Withholding nothing Father. Empty us of all unrighteousness, every unclean thought, every deceitful way, every unrighteous chain. We confess that our hearts have been broken then hardened by our sinful desires, and many times we have tried to hide our uncleanness from you. Our hearts are broken and we cannot save ourselves. Please forgive us for the way our brokenness has caused us to treat others, to treat our own brothers and sisters, our heads and our elders. Thank You for Your correction Father. Fill us with all that You are Father. We thank you for knowing us before our beginnings and our own hearts better than we do. We thank you for choosing us and justifying us for salvation and righteousness in You. We thank you for replacing our hardened and shattered hearts through the power of the Holy Spirit. Please guard our hearts from further damage, and help us to not be discouraged when we feel the emotions and hear the lies of the enemy formed specifically to lead us into doubt. Renew our minds daily and give us assurance through Your promises, Your love, and Your Holy spirit which You sent to us as a Comforter. Father, we confess that we are finished dying for ourselves because outside of You we are not living. We thank you for the opportunity You have provided us through our submission to You that gives us escape from the misery of a self-centered death camouflaged as life in this world. No matter what we now face we know You are with us. Constantly guard our hearts and minds from ever doubting Your unshakable love for us. Help us to always think of the fact that You have made us for Yourself and that we are the apple of Your eye. Lead us to live our lives for You displaying Your will and righteousness wherever we go, and never be ashamed for You are the only thing worth dying for, worth being persecuted for, worth being crucified for. Because You are life and life more abundantly is found only in You. Father we praise you for making us new creatures, that the old man has died and through You every thing in us has become new! We are thankful that You know and judge us rightly by our hearts and our innermost thoughts. Keep us from allowing our past shallow, and worldly judgments of others become barriers in our execution of Your work. Please help us to see others through Your eyes, and in the spirit so we can express the same mercy and grace You have given us. We pray that we continue to grow in our boldness to always be planting seed and be about our Fathers business. Father we thank You for not forgetting our covenant and for reconciling us back to You as You promised. We thank you that although we cannot see the work you are doing we know with all assurance that it is happening at this very moment. We thank you that this work has started in us. We know and stand in assurance that as You prepare us for the union of head to body You are also preparing our heads for their positions in Israel and these holy unions. That although we are meant to follow right now we take the lead, with gladness and humility, as empty vessels hearts, mind, and soul, longing to be filled and used by You. Let us be Your beacons of light . Let us be You overflowing vessels of love that cover all, bear all, and are full of faith. Continue to show us our weaknesses and errs Father. Continue to purify us through your word and render us perfect in your sight. We thank You that You are not only preparing us but providing us with the tools to succeed. You are drawing us towards You more everyday and as we grow closer to You we grow closer to those who belong to You. We long to succeed and fulfill your will Father. Remake us all in the proper image, Father. Tear down the images given to us by the world and replace them with righteousness. Tear down the improper thought patterns and strongholds of the mind and replace them with good, pure, and perfect thoughts . Keep us in line with the Holy spirit. Heal us in our inner most broken places Father that there not be a chink anywhere in our armor for the enemy to infiltrate us again. We pray for Your healing power, Your restoration. You know our needs. You know our desires Father. We no longer pray to consume our lust..we will no longer ask amiss. Let our desires mirror the desires of Your heart. They are Yours and we ask in assurance that all of our needs and desires are being granted. We thank You that we want not because it is done. We claim this era of completion. So be it.

Zechariah 2:8 For thus saith the Lord of hosts; After the glory hath he sent me unto the nations which spoiled you: for he that toucheth you toucheth the apple of his eye.

2 Corinthians 5:17 Therefore if any man be in Christ, he is a new creature: old things are passed away; behold, all things are become new.

Psalms 26:2 Examine me, O LORD, and prove me; try my reins and my heart

James 4 From whence come wars and fightings among you? come they not hence, even of your lusts that war in your members?Ye lust, and have not: ye kill, and desire to have, and cannot obtain: ye fight and war, yet ye have not, because ye ask not.Ye ask, and receive not, because ye ask amiss, that ye may consume it upon your lusts.Ye adulterers and adulteresses, know ye not that the friendship of the world is enmity with God? whosoever therefore will be a friend of the world is the enemy of God.Do ye think that the scripture saith in vain, The spirit that dwelleth in us lusteth to envy?But he giveth more grace. Wherefore he saith, God resisteth the proud, but giveth grace unto the humble.Submit yourselves therefore to God. Resist the devil, and he will flee from you.Draw nigh to God, and he will draw nigh to you. Cleanse your hands, ye sinners; and purify your hearts, ye double minded.Be afflicted, and mourn, and weep: let your laughter be turned to mourning, and your joy to heaviness.Humble yourselves in the sight of the Lord, and he shall lift you up.Speak not evil one of another, brethren. He that speaketh evil of his brother, and judgeth his brother, speaketh evil of the law, and judgeth the law: but if thou judge the law, thou art not a doer of the law, but a judge.There is one lawgiver, who is able to save and to destroy: who art thou that judgest another? Go to now, ye that say, To day or to morrow we will go into such a city, and continue there a year, and buy and sell, and get gain: Whereas ye know not what shall be on the morrow. For what is your life? It is even a vapour, that appeareth for a little time, and then vanisheth away. For that ye ought to say, If the Lord will, we shall live, and do this, or that.But now ye rejoice in your boastings: all such rejoicing is evil. Therefore to him that knoweth to do good, and doeth it not, to him it is sin.